Cherished

Cherished

Heal Your Past, Stop Settling, and Embrace the Love You're Capable Of

Devon Ballard-Hudson

Healing & Homesteading

For my soulmate, Christian
And for Brahm, Branson, and Nevaeh

"Would you like to hear an epic Love story? You, healing from all of it. And living free."
— Jaiya John

To my readers:

This is not like other love stories, but it's a love story that needs to be told, because there are others who need to hear it. It's a little bit messy. The main character doesn't live happily ever after with the first person she falls in love with or even the first person she marries. This is a story of second chances. It is a story about finding a soulmate when you were certain soulmates didn't exist. Above all else, it's a story about healing.

What I love most about this story is that it is true, and it is my own.

Contents

Part I: Seeds

The Catalyst

Sometimes the fog is lifted and for a moment we are able to peer deep into ourselves, and what we find there wakes us up with our own stark, naked truth. Once we see our own truth like that, there's no turning back.

At least that's how it happened for me. It was early November. The cool air and falling leaves, if I slowed down enough to even notice them, were telltale signs of the approaching winter. There is a certain wisdom in nature. She doesn't grasp at what once was, nor does she mourn for her fallen leaves. She just knows when to let go.

As I dashed around the house, hastily grabbing an old notebook and rummaging for a pen that still worked, I reassured my boys, aged two and five, I would be back home in time to tuck them in.

On the drive to my monthly women's circle, I contemplated the theme for the month—the heart's deepest desire. I felt sure my heart's actual deepest desire must be *to be desired*. Why else would I be feeling all these mixed-up emotions lately?

Lying down during our guided meditation, I slowed my breath until my thoughts dispersed and my mind cleared.

Then I heard the leader prompt, "What is your heart's deepest desire?"

Without hesitation from some place inside of me, I heard, "To be cherished."

The answer came so swiftly and without any thought on my own part, I immediately knew it came from my own deep knowing.

Quiet tears fell freely down my cheeks. Though the answer reverberated as true in my entire body, I wasn't sure I liked that answer. Being cherished felt somehow self-indulgent.

Can a wife and mother of two young kids really expect to feel cherished by her husband? I silently wondered.

My mind immediately pushed back with thoughts like, *That's not realistic,* or *Only in the movies.*

It didn't even occur to me at the time, but "to love and to cherish" were literally the promises we had made to each other on our wedding day. Had I really chosen someone who was going to love and cherish me for better or worse, in sickness and in health? Lately I was feeling tolerated at best and criticized at worst, but I definitely hadn't felt cherished.

That night I recited a prayer on the way home, "Even though I can't see a way now, I open myself up to being cherished."

The truth is, for me, winter was approaching—not only in the outer world, but also in my inner world. Old beliefs were beginning to die and fall away, as to make room for my own rebirth.

The Leader with the Tattoos

As I write this now, I'm about a month from my fortieth birthday. There are multiple definitions of "a moment," but one popular answer is that a moment lasts ninety seconds. So technically, I have experienced over thirteen million moments in my life so far. Memory, however, is a fickle friend, and while I don't know the exact percentage, I'm sure I can only recall a fraction of the moments of my life.

That's what makes it so extraordinary that I can vividly recall such an unassuming moment from five years ago, when I stood in the entrance of the downtown Glassworks building and ushered in attendees arriving to our leadership conference.

I can recall exactly what I was wearing: a gray polo shirt with my team's logo on it, black dress pants with tiny white polka dots, and a pair of sensible, tan leather flats. I wore my hair down with a small pin to keep my bangs out of my face.

As I stood there, a group hurried through the door to my left, running a little late for the start of the event. I greeted and pointed them towards the elevator. One of them looked up at me and quickly made eye contact as he rushed to the elevator. His tattoos peeked out from under the arm of his dark blue shirt, and even as he rushed past me, his stride was still somehow calm and collected.

That was it. The moment was over. It couldn't have even been quite ninety seconds from start to finish. It was September 26, 2018, but that's not the beginning of this story, because this is not a story that can be defined with a beginning and an ending as we understand time.

Despite the hundreds of leaders in attendance at our event, I continued to notice *him*, and for the remainder of the day, I lost count of how many times we unintentionally made eye contact.

When the event ended, I made a last-minute decision to drive across town to Whole Foods to pick up a few things and grab a bite to eat.

As I walked towards the entrance, I looked up, and there *he* was again coming out of the store!

The world around me became a little fuzzy. I felt like both my brain and my body were moving in slow motion. As we passed each other, I think I smiled and whispered, "Hi," under my breath, but I can't be sure. I was too busy processing the shock of seeing him again that very same day in a completely different part of town.

He looked just as surprised to see me as I was to see him.

This grabbed my full attention. What was this magnetism I had been palpating all day, and did it somehow manifest by bringing us to the same place at the exact same time? What are the actual odds of that happening completely by chance?

On the surface I already had the perfect life—the husband, the two young kids, the nice house. I had checked off all the boxes. I clearly wasn't looking for anyone, yet there was something about our encounter I just couldn't shake.

The next day at work, I came in and asked my teammates about "the leader with the tattoos." They shrugged me off.

Nobody knew who I was talking about, but I *needed* to

know his name. When an email was later sent to the attendees of the event, my inner detective emerged. I meticulously scrolled over every name in the email, hovering so I could see each person's profile image. I abruptly stopped and narrowed my focus over one of the small, one-by-one-inch images, and there he was looking back at me through the computer screen: Christian Hudson.

Botany

"Seeds never lose their potential, not even in dirt."
— Matshona Dhliwayo

On and off for the months that followed he remained in the back of my mind, even though I couldn't understand why. From what I understand about the science of botany, when a seed is planted it remains inactive until the conditions are right for germination; this is referred to as dormancy. I think that is how it worked for us too. Seeds had been planted that day in September, and as I would learn later, seeds had even been planted years before that day, but the conditions were not yet right for growth.

Remember that picture-perfect life I mentioned? In reality, my picture-perfect life was actually not so perfect. The hardest part of authoring my story has been deciding how much information to share regarding my relationship with my first husband and the father of my two boys, whom from here on out I shall refer to by the pseudonym "Ricardo."

It doesn't feel right to share the intimate details of the relationship, yet I couldn't tell you a complete story if I chose to omit that part of my life completely. It's such an essential part of my story—supposedly having it all and then having it all fall apart, only to be blown away by the love waiting for me on the other side of the end of my former life as I knew it.

Despite my deep desire to feel cherished, I was in a marriage with someone who was unable to verbally express love and affection towards me but *did* express criticism. Like most things in life, there were two sides to our marriage. At our best we had a friendship and someone to share laughs with. At our worst, I walked on eggshells around his moods, feeling like I could never do enough or be enough as a wife.

To avoid feeling the discomfort that came along with holding these two dichotomous beliefs about my partner, I reasoned with myself that this is just what it's like when you've been married a while and the "honeymoon" is over. This is real life, not a fairy tale. Nobody lives happily ever after; well, nobody, except for maybe Johnny Cash and June Carter.

A Frog in Hot Water

There is a popular myth that says if you plunge a frog into boiling water, it will immediately jump out. But if you place the frog into cool water and slowly heat it to boiling, the frog won't notice and will slowly cook to death.

I have no idea why anyone would ever want to boil a live frog. It seems both unnecessary and overly sadistic, but I get the analogy. I was like the frog sitting in a pot of slowly simmering water; things were coming to a boil, but it was so gradual, I hardly noticed. All along there was some small part of me, perhaps my inner voice, who knew things weren't all they should be and that I deserved to feel loved and cherished. I silenced that voice with justifications and platitudes until eventually I convinced myself things really were fine. I had to, because we had two young children, and I needed to believe we could make things work and things would eventually get better.

Instead, after giving birth to my second son, I was confronted with a level of anxiety I had never experienced before. With a background in psychology and health studies, I was both frustrated and perplexed by the way I was feeling. I was supposed to be the "expert" with the answers. Instead, I was at the mercy of my strange and debilitating symptoms:

The constant pit of dread in my stomach, accompanying me like an unwelcome house guest ...

The inability to get a full, satisfying breath, which made me feel like I was losing my mind ...

And worst of all, the sensation of suffocation, which would pop up unexpectedly, and felt like I was drowning from inside my body.

The anxiety was my pot of water, finally boiling over. Years of unaddressed trauma, limiting subconscious beliefs, a covertly toxic partnership, and an unsustainable lifestyle were screaming for my attention, and I was ready to listen.

It was my experience with anxiety that propelled me forward on my healing journey—a journey that would begin to restore me physically, mentally, and spiritually.

Story, Imprints, and Subconscious Beliefs

See for me, I've always looked at anxiety as the body's way of saying, "Something is not right. I don't feel safe." So instead of trying to silence the anxiety with unhealthy coping mechanisms or sedatives, I leaned into the anxiety to see what it was trying to tell me. (Side note: I am not anti-medication. Medication can, and has been for me at times, a useful tool in my healing toolbox. I just didn't want to use meds to numb the pain at the expense of ignoring the message that the pain [the anxiety] was trying to communicate to me.)

I believe, for any of us to heal, we must work through our own story. Aundi Kolber, author of *Try Softer,* defines "story" as the templates that we live from. She describes these templates as "the compilation of events, emotions, sensations, ideas, and relationships we've experienced." Our stories are held in our bodies, and they affect how we see the world. Quite frankly, they shape our entire reality (Kolber, 2020).

I also love how Kimberly Ann Johnson, author of *Call of the Wild,* frames these life experiences as "imprints." Our true self, which is unique to who we are, is referred to as our "blueprint." "As we are born and go through life we acquire imprints," she says. Some of our life experiences, or imprints, are positive and have a way of enhancing our blueprint, but often these imprints are potentially damaging and can lead to disconnection from our true self and create dysfunction in our daily lives (Johnson, 2021).

Compelled by my anxiety, I began the process of understanding my story and how my past was showing up in the present, begging to be healed. One of the most significant parts of my healing journey was the discovery of certain subconscious beliefs, developed in my childhood, that were driving my anxiety.

The subconscious part of our mind does not analyze or reason like the conscious part of our mind does. It simply gathers data from our life experiences and automatically stores it. Thousands of these stored "data points" gathered from experiences when we're young become beliefs that then become rules for our lives. These "rules for our lives" are our subconscious beliefs, forged in childhood, which often rule many of our decisions, emotions, and behaviors as an adult (Scher, 2019). All of this happens without our conscious effort or knowledge.

Regardless of how caring and attentive our parents or other caregivers were, we all gathered and developed limiting subconscious beliefs as children to some extent. Our developing brains were doing their best to make sense of our environment.

How many of us as kids were told to "clean our plates" at dinnertime? We never did help any of those hypothetical starving children; instead, what many of us *did* do was carry a guilt complex about not finishing our food into adulthood that led to perpetual overeating.

Hopefully, you catch my drift. Whether you want to label it as "trauma" or whether you call them templates, imprints, or subconscious beliefs, we have gathered them throughout our life, and like an overpacked suitcase, we are still carrying them around with us today.

Until I owned my story, until I discovered and healed myself from limiting, subconscious beliefs like "I am not enough" or "I don't deserve to be unconditionally loved," I would remain stuck in situations that reflected these beliefs back to me.

These beliefs were the template running in the background of my life and my marriage. Of course, if I believed I was never enough, I would end up with a partner who would reflect that back to me.

To Heal

"Don't turn away. Keep your gaze on the bandaged place. That is where the light enters you."
— Rumi

The word "heal" can be defined in multiple ways, but my favorite is simply "to restore to original purity or integrity" (Merriam-Webster, 2022). Much of the healing work I reference throughout this book is simply a returning to a part of us that is already pure and whole.

In the quote above, Rumi advises us to keep our gaze on the bandaged place. Our "bandaged places" —our trauma, grief, emotional pain, and discomfort are all pointing us toward that which in ourselves needs healing. No amount of self-care, medication, or even meditation will be enough to restore us if we are using these modalities to bury the pain. Don't bury it; keep your gaze on it. The healing journey is *through* our pain, not *around* it.

As for my journey, I had a lot of work to do. I began

acknowledging the things from my past that had inadvertently created self-limiting beliefs for me, including the acknowledgment that as a young child, the stringent religious environment I was exposed to was traumatic for me and left me with some pretty dysfunctional imprints.

I acknowledged my past experiences while beginning to forge new, healthier spiritual beliefs of my own. I made peace with God as I understood her. This deep work was part of my germination process and was necessary before any seeds that had been planted would be ready for growth.

Synchronicity

Carl Jung first introduced the concept of synchronicity, which he eventually defined as "meaningful coincidence of two or more events where something other than the probability of chance is involved". If you have ever found yourself asking, "What are the chances?" you have probably just experienced a synchronicity. I like to think of synchronicities as the tiny miracles in everyday life.

I have always noticed and appreciated plenty of synchronicities in my life, like the time when the Kentucky Derby fell on my friend Emily's birthday the first year after she had passed away from cancer.

I placed my bet on a horse with formidable 65:1 odds—practically an impossibility in terms of horse racing. I chose the horse strictly based on its name, Country House, because I met Emily through her business, The Diaper Fairy Cottage. A country house and a cottage seemed similar enough, so this was the horse I picked to honor her birthday, despite its horrible odds.

As it should have, the horse with the best odds that year came in first, or so it seemed. In what the *LA Times* described as the most incredible post-running of the Kentucky Derby, Maximum Security was disqualified for interference, and Country House was declared the winner of the 145th running of the Kentucky Derby. It was the first on-track disqualification in the history of the race (Cherwa, 2019). I donated all my winnings to the scholarship fund that had just been set up in her memory.

That, my friends, is synchronicity.

My and Christian's run-in at Whole Foods that day was just the first of many more synchronous moments to come. I should warn you the events I will detail in the pages to follow are sprinkled with so much synchronicity, you may come to the inevitable conclusion that a force stronger than us—God, the Universe, the Flow of Goodness, or whatever holy name you ascribe—was most definitely the orchestrator.

Steadfastness

"On the nights you feel outnumbered, baby, I'll be out there somewhere .... How long can you wait for the one you deserve?"

— Dermot Kennedy, "Outnumbered"

For Christian, this story begins four years before our Whole Foods encounter, in 2014, the year I won a major award for the company we work for.

Christian happened to be attending the conference where my award video was about to debut. It had been a long day of listening to speakers, one right after the other, with little breaks in between, and Christian doodled on the pen and paper in front of him, justifiably zoning out a bit.

My award video started playing across the big screen at the front of the room, and something about my voice caused him to look up at the screen. That is when he saw me for the first time. He was immediately captivated, his first thought being, *This girl can't be real.*

Growing up, I used to joke about becoming famous one day. As it turns out, I was *just* famous enough to get on the big screen for *just* long enough for him to notice me, and while I may never win any Oscars, that is more than enough fame for me. Because, you see, that day the seeds of what was to come years later had been planted.

A few weeks after seeing me on the big screen, my actual realness became quite apparent when he saw me walking, or should I say waddling, down the hallway of our work building, *real* and *really* pregnant.

That should have been enough to kill any romantic notion he felt; nevertheless, he kept an admiring eye on me from a distance.

When three years later, in 2017, I was once again pregnant, he wrote me off as "likely happily married to an ex-fraternity boy, who grew up to be a successful businessman or doctor, living in a nice, big house in the suburbs" (his actual words). If I may quote En Vogue, he knew at that point he was "never gonna get it, never gonna get it." But even as he wrote me off as unavailable, he held on to his admiration for me at a distance and still viewed me as his dream girl ... in another life.

I assumed the first time we saw each other was the moment I vividly recall making eye contact with him in 2018. Knowing what I know now, I find it oddly comforting—his steadfast, secret affection towards me. It somehow makes the time I spent locking myself in the bathroom, crying and feeling unappreciated and overwhelmed, less sad—just knowing that he was out there somewhere feeling that way toward me, and that we would eventually, inevitably collide.

For all my *Office* fans, it's like that episode where Michael Scott suddenly taps into his deep inner wisdom after missing his chance with his love interest, Holly, at the company picnic. He just smiles at the camera and calmly reflects, "I think we're one of those couples who'll have a long story when people ask how we found each other. I will see her every now and then, and maybe one year she'll be with somebody and the next year I'll be with somebody, and it's gonna take a long time ... and then it's perfect. I'm in no rush."

Maybe you're someone who would find it comforting too —to know there is no need for urgency to find your soulmate now, or by the time you're thirty-five, or whatever arbitrary deadline you or the world has imposed. What's yours will make its way to you.

If Christian and I had known we were to have been together, we might have forced things at the wrong time, afraid to miss our opportunity, but I didn't have to panic or force things. All I did was my deep, personal inner healing work and let life unfold naturally, like that dormant seed buried deep in the ground awaiting its time to germinate and eventually bloom.

Nature's timeline is outlandishly patient and perfectly wise. Who are we to question the Universe's timing? In our natural world some seeds can remain buried in their soil for more than fifty years before germination; yet we pressure ourselves to find love, start a family, or figure out our life's purpose all by some arbitrary timeline living in our head.

The Struggle

You may be wondering by now, "How could you allow yourself to feel attracted towards another man while still married?"

Fair question. Life is often messy, and the truth is not always black and white. Sometimes it's spattered with areas of gray. This was definitely one of those gray areas.

I would not call what I felt towards Christian a sexual attraction. It was deeper than that. It was more a sense of magnetism. He piqued my interest, and I wasn't sure why; we had never even spoken.

"Feeling attracted to someone else" (outside of my long-standing crush on actor Tom Hardy) was a *symptom* of my distressed marriage. It was not the *cause* of my distressed marriage. I didn't consciously choose to feel this way, and there was a struggle inside of me to fight the feelings.

At first I just wrote it off as my need for attention or to feel desired. I tried to avoid scolding myself for the way I was feeling, but instead I got curious and sought to understand what my feelings were telling me. Most importantly, I trusted myself.

I knew I had no plans of impulsively acting on my feelings, so I simply let what I was feeling be there. I asked myself questions, and I decided to listen and trust the information provided back to me. Willing myself to feel any other way would have backfired. I have found the more I try to push something away, typically the stronger its power grows—what we resist, persists. Besides, telling myself how I *should* feel is called "shoulding," and I believe you must never "should" on yourself or anyone else for that matter.

Time to Get Those Steps In

"I used to dream that you would talk to me."
— Dermot Kennedy, "For Island Fires and Family"

The months passed by and soon it had been a year since my and Christian's first encounter when I unexpectedly started seeing him every day in the lobby of our work building during my afternoon walks. I felt the strong urge to strike up a conversation with him, but wondered, *Will he even remember me, or am I making a bigger deal of that day than what it really was?*

On one of my walks, I noticed him sitting at a table with my friend, Byron. I finished my walk and headed five floors up to my cubicle, but no sooner had I sat down at my desk than I realized, *Here's my chance!*

After more than a year of wondering about our mystifying encounter, I now had an excuse to stop and talk with

Byron, and in the process introduce myself to Christian. The only things standing between us now were five floors and my wavering confidence.

My heart raced as I rode down the shaky elevator, passed through the buzzing fluorescent lights of the corridor, and back to the lobby. When I approached, I noticed from a distance Byron was already gone. There Christian sat alone at the table, deep in concentration, working on his laptop. My plan had failed. I turned right back around and made the trek back to my desk, feeling like a fool.

Like clockwork, the next day he was there again at the same place.

Each lap, I nervously passed him, deciding whether to try making eye contact. I eventually decided, *Yes, eye contact would definitely be good.*

He must have been plotting to do the same because when I looked up at him, he flashed a welcoming smile and said something to me.

But what did he say?

Because I was wearing earbuds, I had no idea what he said, but before my brain had time to process what my body was doing, I was pulling my earbuds out and walking directly over to the table to talk to him as if it was an involuntary bodily function taking over.

Shaking on the inside, I tried to make casual conversation that sounded normal. Because of this I recall little about what was discussed, but we proceeded to carry on a nice conversation as if we were old friends. We talked about my Halloween costume, our kids, his favorite comedian. We could have been discussing gas prices or the rate of inflation in Indonesia for all I cared. He talked to me! I floated back to my desk a new woman, a cheesy smile on my face that made my coworkers wonder what was up with me.

Oh, and by the way, "Time to get those steps in?" was the first thing he said to me.

Soon after our conversation, I attended my women's group that fateful day in November, the one focused on the theme of the heart's deepest desire. So it makes sense I entered that sacred circle troubled by my conflicting emotions.

Cherished—that was the directive that had bubbled up from inside of me, and its truth would not leave me alone. Knowing this truth that had been spoken from that authentic place deep within me, I could no longer allow myself to go back to not being cherished, to not feeling loved.

Truth Hurts

If you know anything about pop music in 2019, then you know about Lizzo's "Truth Hurts." "Why men great till they gotta be great?" Touché Lizzo, touché.

A friend of mine created a "Truth Hurts" parody for her real-estate business, and so just for fun, I also took a stab at it, rewriting the lyrics to describe the work my team does at the company I work for. For example:

Lizzo's verse:

> You coulda had a bad bitch, non-committal
> Help you with your career, just a little
> You're supposed to hold me down

But you're holding me back
And that's the sound of me not calling you back
My version:

You coulda had a bad job, detrimental
Nothing like a career, with potential
But you got hired here
There's no holding you back
And that's the sound recruiter calling you back

I'll admit, it was over-the-top cheesy, but the lyrics were spot-on, and my boss decided we should produce a music video for it to play at our end-of-year celebration scheduled for the following week. The end-of-year celebration at my workplace is where everyone showcases their teams' accomplishments, accompanied by humorous homemade videos to get the point across.

I loved the idea of creating a video, but it was the day before Thanksgiving, almost no one was even in the office, and we only had one week until the event. The chances of finding anyone with the skills and the time to record and produce a music video that week were pretty slim. However, that day I had a meeting with Byron. I explained my predicament to him and asked if he knew of anyone who could produce a video for me. His immediate response: "Let me see if Christian Hudson is in the office today."

This is another one of those *"What are the chances?"* moments. Of the thousands of people who work in the building—it had to be him. I was officially a nervous wreck because—a little backstory—I happened to discover after some slick Facebook "research" (that's millennial speak for social media stalking) that Christian was a local hip-hop artist who went by the name Nacirema, and he was, like, *really* good. Like "had just opened for the Wu-Tang Clan the month before" good.

Imagine you say to your friend, "I just tried this new beef Wellington recipe, I've never made it before, do you know anyone who would like to try it?"

To which your friend responds, "Oh yeah, let me get Gordon Ramsay up here real quick."

That is the amount of pressure I suddenly came under.

Within minutes Christian was in the tiny meeting room with Bryon and me. He strode in with the same calm, confident composure I remembered, which was apparently his trademark. I nervously messed with my hair as he listened to my homemade parody, which included witty lyrics and my feeble attempts at rapping, all of which was produced with a cheap karaoke app on my phone while I was driving in the car on my way to pick up my kids. (Please don't try this at home.)

He was super gracious about the request and agreed to meet with me the Monday after Thanksgiving to get the video recorded. Throughout the entire process, he was kind, accommodating, and a complete gentleman. All I needed was one good excuse to dismiss that mystical experience we had shared the year before. If he would have been rude, sleazy, or disrespectful, I could get on with my life. But of course, he had to be practically perfect.

The music video is published on YouTube, and for those who are curious, it can be found by Googling "Truth Hurts, PPS Culture Edition." I often go back and watch our video just to marvel at how utterly clueless we both were. We had no idea we would soon permanently change each other's lives in the best way possible.

Options

A woman I know recently broke off her engagement with her partner of seven years, just one month before their destination wedding that dozens of friends and family had made travel arrangements to attend. She knew he wasn't right for her, and so she did what most would never do, which was risk disappointing everyone so she would not disappoint herself. This may have been the hardest decision she ever had to make, but it was the right one. I admire her bravery and resilience. She did not settle.

Someone else recently told me my love story had inspired her to cut ties with a gentleman she had been seeing off and on since her divorce. He was not "the one," and she knew that in her gut. She also chose not to settle.

I don't know what kind of impact hearing my love story might have on you, but I do know this. Knowing what I know now, we all have two options, and here is what they are:

Option 1: You do you: passionately create the best life possible for yourself and for your loved ones (or children if you happen to have them). Do the work. Seek therapy. Heal old wounds. Deepen your spirituality. Focus on your healing and then go out and help heal others. Leave your mark on this world, no matter how small it seems. Start checking off your bucket list. None of this is selfish. Your happiness is contagious and spills out onto those around you. Create a life of radical self-love that just leaks out on everyone around you ... *without a romantic partner.*

Option 2: All the above, enriched by your soulmate.

How will you know if you've found your soulmate? I can't pretend to speak for everyone, but I would venture to say if you are questioning whether or not you are with your soulmate, then she or he may not be your soulmate. If you just rolled your eyes at the idea of a soulmate, then I would also venture to say you have not found your soulmate.

When Christian and I eventually indulged our spark and began our journey as a couple, I knew from a deep-down place I had found my one. The cliché I had heard all my life was "you'll just know when it's right," but I had never believed the hype.

I thought soulmates were outright fiction. I believed you just found someone with whom you were compatible enough, then you decided whether to stay with this person. I didn't think you could possibly just *know*, until I did *just know*.

When you find your person, you won't have to play a strategic game of chess where each player makes sure to never give too much and to always keep the upper hand. You won't have to beg, borrow, and steal for this person's affection.

While the dictionary may identify a soulmate as, "a person ideally suited to another as a close friend or romantic partner," I can't give you an operational definition of soulmate. It's an essence that can't be properly bottled with words, but it will be the kind of love and connection that just fits; there's no forcing it.

If radical love and passion is something that you want in your life, you can have it. I can't tell you when or how it will show up. There are no rules or timeline to these things, but the love you've dared to imagine for yourself—you can have it. There is someone out there who will give you love and receive the love you give in ways that exceed all your expectations.

The trick is to never settle, and therefore I have NOT listed a third option for you. The third option is settling, and if you've picked up this book and made it this far, then from this point forward, settling is no longer an option for you. You either live your amazing life solo or with your soulmate. There is no other alternative.

I don't know you personally, so you may be wondering how *I* could know what is possible for *you*. Here is what I do know. I know what it is like to have settled, and I also know what it is like to experience a love that is so transformative and true, you give thanks every day just because it exists, and it happened to you. I am just an ordinary woman who decided I deserved to be loved and cherished, and if it can happen for me, it can happen for anyone.

There are lots of reasons we settle. Maybe it's fear that the biological clock is ticking because your friends have settled down and begun having children. Perhaps you haven't learned to love yourself enough to just be with yourself, so you find someone to fill the empty space in the bed next to you. For some, unhealed wounds force you into sabotage mode when love does show up for you. Maybe it's just that you've convinced yourself the love you desire doesn't actually exist. Or, if you're anything like I was, it's a combination of all of the above.

These stories we tell ourselves don't even necessarily originate from our own mind, but rather, they are transmitted to us from our families, friends, upbringing, or culture. Many times, we limit ourselves to what we saw modeled in our home growing up, but this is your life, not theirs. You are the author of your own story. Please remember your options.

Also, while you're busy not settling, enjoying your incredible life, keep in mind you are under no obligation to put any part of your life on hold waiting for a partner. You are not an old-school Disney princess; you are a complete and whole being just as you are. Great love is already all around you. As author Victoria Erickson so eloquently puts it, "Consider soulmates to also be in the form of friends and animals, the wind, the tides, the plants, pieces of art, and the moon."

Death by One Thousand Cuts

So, back to the story. After we recorded my "Truth Hurts" parody, there were a few video-related emails or IMs exchanged between me and Christian, but we ran out of professional reasons to correspond with one another and our line of communication fizzled out.

By December of 2019, I knew I was at a breaking point in my marriage. I was still troubled and confused by the attraction I felt towards Christian. Looking for answers, I began reading a book by Esther Perel called *Mating in Captivity*. The book examines the inverse relationship between domesticity and sexual desire and explains what it takes to bring desire into the marriage (Perel, 2007).

Throughout our relationship, I had initiated counseling with Ricardo on a couple occasions, although we only ever completed a handful of sessions. I studied Gary Chapman's "love languages." I told him what mine were and tried understanding how I could more effectively communicate in his love languages.

I familiarized myself with John Gottman's work, which is considered the gold standard for researched-based marriage interventions. These were all things I had initiated, with his reaction ranging from little interest to complete denial of any issues. It seemed as though our problems were mostly in my head.

I tried everything I knew to make things better. Since I had reached the point of experiencing feelings for another man, a practically unforgivable impropriety in the eyes of society, I turned to Perel's book, desperately hoping maybe the issue was that we needed to rekindle the fire, and so I threw myself into this last-ditch effort.

The next month or so contained a series of pleasant distractions—closing on a new house, my birthday, and Christmas. We moved into the new house on New Year's Day, 2020.

For most, New Year's represents a new beginning, a chance to start over. In my case, this New Year's would be the start of the end. I'll never forget that day because something happened which, looking back, was the thousandth cut that turned out to be fatal.

You see, there were times in our marriage when I told

Ricardo I felt the seemingly small emotional hurts I absorbed would eventually equate to "death by a thousand cuts." A small paper cut could practically go unnoticed, but one thousand raw paper cuts would be excruciating. It's never one single thing. It's the culmination of all the things.

Our loved ones are going to hurt us. Yes, even your soulmate will hurt you at times. The survival of the relationship is dependent upon what John Gottman refers to as "repair attempts." The Gottman Institute describes a repair attempt as "any statement or action—silly or otherwise—that prevents negativity from escalating out of control" (Brittle, 2022). So, when we hurt our partner, we do something to repair the hurt. We don't leave our partner with an open wound, no matter how minor the cut may seem.

He didn't hurl a ton of horrible insults at me or call me a four-letter word. It was only a single, underhanded remark. I later told him how hurtful it was, but he stood by his words. I refer to this as the fatal cut because looking back that's when my heart checked out. Whether I consciously knew it at that moment, I was done trying.

Explore, Exploit

When I say I was done trying, I'm not saying I had intentionally weighed out all the pros and cons of staying versus leaving and come to a calculated, logical decision. Like I said, I don't think at that point I had even consciously decided the marriage was over. It was more like a switch flipped—my broken spirit knew I was not going to receive what I needed there, nor was there anything left within me to give.

Emily and Amelia Nagoski, co-authors of *Burnout*, would refer to this phenomenon as an "explore/exploit" moment. As they describe in their book, this phenomenon happens naturally in nature. Let's say a squirrel is exploring a certain area of the forest for food (exploit), but as time goes on he begins to find fewer and fewer acorns. There comes a point in his little squirrel brain when he knows he has foraged all he can from this area of the forest, and he moves on (explore) (Nagoski, 2020). He doesn't cling to what once was. He definitely doesn't say to himself, "Hmm ... I know I found acorns here before, so I should stay here longer and hopefully things will get better."

As an animal, the squirrel intuitively knows when he needs to leave. This is mostly not the case for humans because we have this little thing called consciousness, and our life situations are infinitely more complex than a squirrel searching for a nut. Lucky squirrels.

I am *not* saying we should exploit a relationship until we've drained it of everything useful, only to move on to greener pastures. I *am* saying there are countless complex reasons we spend far longer in futile situations, to our own detriment —whether that be a friendship, romantic relationship, job, or other life situation. Most of these reasons boil down to "shoulding" on ourselves:

"I *should* keep this job, at least until the economy gets stronger."

"We *should* stay together for the kids."

"We've been friends since fourth grade, so I *should* be there for her."

We can easily convince ourselves to stay in a situation that is harmful to our overall well-being.

It would ultimately be months before I would consciously make the decision that I wanted out of my marriage, but looking back, I can pinpoint exactly when my spirit made that decision for me. Chances are, there are situations in your life right now where important decisions need to be made. Listen closely; if you can stop shoulding on yourself for a moment, you might find your spirit has already made the decision for you.

Own Your Stuff

"Do the best you can until you know better. Then when you know better, do better."

— Maya Angelou

In telling my story, it is important not to portray myself as some kind of victim. My first marriage was not able to go the distance. By now I have shared enough details to make it apparent it was not a healthy relationship, but I also want to make it clear I don't view myself as a victim.

I'm not sure who said it, but it's been said, "Let's heal so we can stop accidentally hurting people we want to love."

I believe my ex loved me the best he could, as much as he was capable, yet I was still hurting; perhaps he was too. I cannot make the decision for another person to heal, but I can choose it for myself, and I did.

Remember, our stories are the templates covertly running our lives. If unhealthy narratives are running our lives, unless we consciously unearth those stories and invest the time in healing and learning new and healthier ways of being in the world, we will continue unintentionally inflicting pain upon ourselves or others.

Elements of my past—and the corresponding subconscious beliefs that went along with those parts of my story—played a significant role in my first marriage. I was still healing the "not enough" script. I was a chronic people-pleaser, letting fear of disappointing others and feeling overly responsible for others' emotions dictate a lot of my actions.

On the surface I expected to be treated well, but on a deeper, energetic level, that was not what I was attracting. I would feel angry and defensive when I perceived I was not being loved and appreciated, but what I didn't understand is that my subconscious beliefs about myself carried an energy, and that energy was like a radio frequency. If I didn't like the music, I needed to change the channel by changing my energy.

I consider one of my first spiritual teachers to have been Iyanla Vanzant, who I discovered in my mid-twenties when a friend let me borrow her 1998 book *In the Meantime*. This is where I was first introduced to the concept of "owning my own stuff," nearly fifteen years ago. Clearly, this is a lifelong process.

To own one's stuff, we have to own the role we play in our relationships. Vanzant explains,

> Sooner or later, we must all accept the fact that in

a relationship, the only person you are dealing with is yourself. Your partner does nothing more than reveal your stuff to you. Your fear! Your anger! Your pattern! Your craziness! As long as you insist on pointing the finger out there, at them, you will continue to miss out on the divine opportunity to clear your stuff. (Vanzant, 1998)

You see, I would be totally justified if I wanted to bask in my anger or sulk in self-pity at how I was sometimes treated by my ex, but I choose not to. I know I walked into that relationship and ultimately entered that marriage with eyes wide open. I came in with my own set of subconscious rules, a lifetime of imprints, and my own stories. I was the one responsible for setting and enforcing the standard for how I expected to be treated. How, then, can I be angry at someone else for what I allowed?

It's not, "How could he do this to me?!" but, "Why did I do this to myself?"

In her book, *Yesterday I Cried*, Vanzant says,

You can accept or reject the way you are treated by other people, but until you heal the wounds of your past, you will continue to bleed. You can bandage the bleeding with food, with alcohol, with drugs, with work, with cigarettes, with sex, but eventually, it will all ooze through and stain your life. You must find the strength to open the wounds, stick your hands inside, pull out the core of the pain that is holding you in your past, the memories, and make peace with them. (Vanzant, 1998)

My ex's story is not mine to tell. I cannot say what his experience was like in our marriage. I cannot know what in his story needs healing. All I know is, for me, our marriage became emotionally toxic. Thankfully, liberation is a two-way street. When we did eventually decide to divorce, we both experienced a sense of relief when the decision had been made to go our separate ways.

Nowadays, my ex and I are much better as co-parents, and apparently even my now six-year-old, who was only two when we separated, agrees. A couple Thanksgivings ago when asked for three things he was thankful for, he replied, "Halloween, my birthday, and for when we got two houses."

A marriage that comes to its conclusion isn't a failure. Staying in a toxic relationship and modeling that toxicity for your children is.

I strongly believe in the words of Maya Angelou when she said people do the best they can until they know better, then when they know better, they do better. And I know we can do better, and that is why we must heal. If you want to attract a partner that is whole, you have to work on being whole. Like attracts like.

Darkness

"Sometimes when you're in a dark place you think you've been buried, but you've actually been planted."
— Christine Caine

Christian and I deepened our budding friendship over the first couple months of 2020 as we worked on another video project together. While we began to recognize we had lots in common, he was always completely professional and respectful. He was also kind—*surprisingly* kind.

Once, after a meeting, we were both waiting for our elevator. The elevators are so slow, it's almost as if the elevator technology has remained untouched since the building was originally constructed in 1880. Because we were going to different floors in the building, we were taking two different elevators. His elevator came and went at least a couple of times, but he chose to stay with me until my elevator arrived so I would not have to wait alone.

That was enough to make me believe chivalry was not dead, and I couldn't delude myself into thinking he was being kind for ulterior motives, because I witnessed him being equally kind to the cafeteria workers who served up lunch each day. There is a reason why they say a person who is nice to you but not nice to the server is not a nice person. He treated everyone he encountered as if they were genuinely important to him. I watched as he left each of the lunch ladies with an authentic smile. I was delightfully bemused.

Like a true (elder) millennial, I had taken my time to do some soft internet research to learn a little more about him. Over the course of my social-media scrolling, I found we had some striking similarities. First, we were both born on our grandmother's birthday. Second, according to one post I came across, he and his significant other met, became engaged, and married within one to two months of when Ricardo and I also met, became engaged, and married. Upon discovering this, I felt like I was in the twilight zone, where Christian and I had been obliviously living parallel lives, under the same roof at work, without even knowing each other.

Regardless of how I might have been feeling, knowing he was married, I took care to keep our working relationship professional and platonic. I directed all my focus towards the issue at hand—my feelings of desperation about my marriage.

My biggest concern was my children. No matter how badly I wanted out, it made me sick to think about splitting my boys' childhoods between two houses. I felt stuck. I thought, *I brought these children into the world. How could I dare do this to them?*

Slowly, I started opening myself to the concept of conscious uncoupling—the ending of a romantic relationship or marriage in a respectful, positive, and constructive way (Thomas, 2009). I wanted to believe there was a peaceful way for us to separate that focused on putting our children first.

For the first time I started to confide in those closest to me, my mother and my best friend, how unhappy I was and why. I confided that I had held in and hidden my unhappiness from those I love for a long time because I didn't want to speak poorly of my spouse and taint their opinion of him. Plus, there was a part of me that was ashamed to admit I was in an unhappy marriage. Being a positive person who has always cared about doing my best in all areas of my life, I was reluctant to admit, even to myself, my marriage was "not good."

Paralyzed with fear at the thought of initiating a conversation with Ricardo, I journaled daily planning what I might say. I lost sleep, waking up in the middle of the night having imaginary conversations in my head with him.

I agonized over the imagined disapproval and disappointment of those closest to me, especially Ricardo and my two boys. Contemplating the demise of a marriage and the splitting of a family is a dark place to be. I wasn't sure where to begin, and I sure as hell couldn't see the light at the end of the tunnel just yet.

Darkness serves a purpose both in the natural world and in our inner world. While all seeds need water, oxygen, and proper temperature to develop, some seeds actually require darkness rather than light to germinate. So it is for us humans as well. Much of our deepest and most meaningful growth happens in dark periods of our life.

The revelation of my desire to be cherished was a gift. It gifted me the fortitude to contemplate some much-needed changes in my life, but it didn't always feel like a gift—*sometimes it felt as though I was being buried.* Turns out I had been planted.

As I wrestled internally with all of this, in early March of 2020, the entire world came to a standstill as our lives were flipped upside down due to the onset of the COVID-19 pandemic. Schools closed, workers were sent home to work, and nonessential businesses were forced to close. There was nothing to do but to stay home and face this head on.

The Untaming

During those early quarantine days, a long-time friend of mine called. "I just finished reading this book. I think you would really like it," she said. "It's a Reese's Book Club pick."

I knew nothing about the book she was recommending, so when I confided in her that my marriage was in deep trouble, she jokingly cautioned me to "read the book at my own risk."

The book she recommended was Glennon Doyle's *Untamed*. If you aren't familiar with Glennon, according to *People*, she is the "patron saint of female empowerment," and I'd have to agree.

We've all heard the expression, "When the student is ready, the teacher will appear." Her book couldn't have come at a more opportune time. It's as if the Universe had just dropped the instruction manual for my life into my lap. *Untamed* gave me permission to look within and to trust my instincts, rather than to look outside of myself to what the world expected of me. The pages of her book were like a permission slip, allowing me to move forward with the difficult conversations and decisions that lay ahead.

If you are familiar with the book, it's even uncanny how similar Glennon and Abby's story is to Christian and me. Glennon was in a troubled marriage. She met Abby at a conference. She immediately felt a sense of magnetism towards her. She toiled over whether she could leave her husband and what impact that would have on her kids. So, how odd my friend who knew nothing about what I was going through would call me up and randomly recommend *this* book. Scratch that—it wasn't odd. It was serendipitous, a tiny miracle of sorts.

Glennon's words woke me up with the seemingly obvious realization that we can't keep deluding ourselves with the thought "maybe in another life," as if we get another life. We don't. This is it, and because this is it, we must make big, hard decisions to create the truest, most beautiful life possible for ourselves.

Isn't it silly how we let our fear of disappointing others or fear of others' judgment keep us from making the decision we ultimately know is right? How could I look outside myself for validation that I was making the right decision when no one else had lived inside my skin, when no one else could possibly know what it was like inside the four walls of my marriage?

The decision to end the marriage was the hardest decision I've ever had to make. Perhaps the biggest gift Glennon gave me was her enlightened definition of a broken family: "A broken family is a family in which any member must break herself into pieces to fit in. A whole family is one in which each member can bring her full self to the table knowing that she will always be both held and free" (Doyle, 2020).

Kitchen Appliances

One side effect of buying and moving into a new house during a pandemic shutdown is kitchen appliances become annoyingly hard to procure. By month two of COVID lockdown, Ricardo and I had peacefully made the decision that our marriage had run its course, and I was in the process of moving out. I needed a refrigerator for my new house, but at this point refrigerators were backordered for months.

Since transitioning to full-time work at home during the pandemic, Christian and I were no longer working together on video projects, but I still had his phone number. I knew he had been working part-time at a retailer that sells appliances. Selfishly, I wanted to hear from him, and conveniently my need to locate a kitchen appliance gave me a good excuse to call him, and so I did.

Remember how I said our path to each other was full of synchronicities? Here is another major one. Get ready to have your mind blown just a little. No, he couldn't get me a re-frigerator any sooner, but I learned on that phone call that he was also going through a divorce and had just recently moved into his own apartment.

This now meant the stranger who curiously crossed my path coming out of the grocery store a year and a half earlier had been, for the last ten years, mirroring my life almost exactly, from meeting a significant other, to getting engaged, then married, and now getting divorced and moving into a new home. Each of these significant life milestones had oc-curred at the same time, give or take a month or two.

This little piece of information changed everything. Now, the seeds that had been planted a year and half earlier were ready, after a period of dormancy, to begin to grow.

Part II: Growth

It's in His Kiss

The first time Christian and I kissed, it was as if we stepped through a portal from which there was no turning back. Does that sound extreme? Well, it was. There was nothing ordinary about the kiss, just as there was nothing ordinary about our collective suppressed longing that led up to this moment. There certainly was nothing ordinary about the previous ten years we had spent as strangers, with our personal lives somehow mirroring one another's.

He said something. I don't remember what he said. I remember he stepped closer to me, pulled me in, and kissed me with an intensity that surprised me. I surprised myself with the intensity in which I kissed him back.

It is said the best kiss is one that has already been exchanged a thousand times between the eyes before it reaches the lips. In that moment I relived the first time our eyes locked. I saw his gaze meeting mine as we passed each other coming out of Whole Foods. I saw the almost-sad look in his eyes when I caught him watching me from across the courtyard at work the summer before, and I saw how his eyes had come to light up in recent months when we would cross paths in our daily lives at work. I saw all of it, simultaneously, and it all combusted within the fire of that kiss.

I say we crossed a portal because, like some kind of sacred rite of passage, there was no turning back from that moment, and I wouldn't have wanted to. I had been waiting my whole life to be kissed like that, by this person, whether I had consciously known it or not.

Lockdown Love Letters

Since we both were going through divorces during the time of the initial wave of the coronavirus shutdown in 2020, we had limited opportunities to see each other. We began messaging each other throughout the day, and we quickly learned about the feelings we had both been suppressing for each other—for him as far back as six years.

Those early weeks of us writing to each other will always be some of my most treasured memories. The connection we shared from the beginning was so pure. There were never any games or power struggles like individuals often experience when they first start dating and are feeling each other out. You know how it goes—no one wants to show their hand too early by being more emotionally invested or vulnerable than they perceive the other person is being. We often protect our hearts when meeting someone new by playing these games which serve to keep a tidy fence around our hearts, never revealing or giving too much for fear of being rejected or taken advantage of.

With Christian, even right from the beginning, I always

sensed my heart was safe. Both the magnitude of our connection and the time spent suppressing it resulted in an outpouring of honesty, vulnerability, and affection.

I had been living in an affection desert for years. Now suddenly I was with someone who so naturally and powerfully expressed his feelings for me, and because I was a woman who had done the work, I knew my worth. I was ready to accept this kind of love into my life because deep down I finally knew I was fully worthy of it. I knew *this* is what I had always wanted and needed in a partner. I knew *this* is how I deserved to be treated.

In my gut I trusted what we had, but my head would sometimes interfere with thoughts like, *What if he's too good to be true?*

One day I confessed this fear to him and wrote, "Please don't be this good to me unless you think you can *always* be this good to me."

As I hit send, tears welled in my eyes. Sharing this with him showed me how much I had already emotionally invested in him. I had completely written off a guy like him existing, and now that I knew he was real, I couldn't imagine ever going back to the way things were.

He immediately responded with reassurance, telling me he understood my concerns. "What I can tell you is what I say is genuine and authentic. Of course, actions speak louder than words, but I can give you both, but please know that I totally respect your thoughts and fear and will do all I can to ease that fear," he assured me.

"I can feel that authenticity from you, and I trust you," I told him.

Choosing to listen to your heart can be hard because you must be conscious enough to see past the lens of all your past experiences. In the past, in our mind, is where our triggers lie.

I was dealing with a genuinely good man with whom I had no doubt, even early on, I would be spending my life with. Still, my head and my heart were having it out.

My head desperately wanted to make sense of what was happening, when really it made no sense at all. Who falls in love with their soulmate amid a divorce?! That seems risky and crazy fast, and it might have been, if I hadn't been on a healing journey for years, unknowingly preparing myself for this exact time.

Meanwhile, regardless of what my head was trying to tell me, my heart was already blissfully doodling his name in my notebook.

He understood my feelings and committed to easing my fears, and as it turned out, my heart was 100% right. I could trust him. After thirty-six years, I had finally found a safe place for my heart to land with another person.

As the writing continued, each day he began sending me a note in the morning with a new reason or two why he found me to be amazing. Eventually, the daily reason I was amazing would turn into the daily reason he loves me.

Each night he painted a picture with his words, describing how we would hypothetically fall asleep in each other's arms that given night if we were actually physically together.

"My arms wrap around you tight. I softly kiss your neck

as you are kissing the top of my head. I close my arms around you and tell you how beautiful you are and that I love you more and more each day. I pull you in closer for one last hug and welcome my dreams as they keep me company until we meet again in the morning," he would write to me.

In between us beginning and ending the day together in words, we got to know each other deeply. He continued sending me a daily note with a new reason he loved me until he reached reason number 365, which, spoiler alert, unintentionally turned out to be the day that we eloped.

There Is No Map

I consider myself an emotionally intelligent human being, so I'm well aware that most people in my life, and perhaps even some now reading this book, were skeptical or concerned about me moving on so quickly after my divorce. Even those who love me the most may have been worried I was not in a good spot emotionally to immediately move into a committed relationship, and there were others who flat-out disapproved.

The "me" of five or ten years ago would have been crushed by the worry and weight of others' disapproval. My former self would have sought out popular opinion to get some sort of external validation that what I was doing was ok, but I had spent the entirety of my life, that I can recall, trying to please others and seeking external validation. This time was different. This time I had learned to quit looking externally, and to go within. Free from what society expected of me, I listened to my intuition. I trusted myself. Whether it made sense to anyone else or not, once Christian and I got to know each other, we both knew we had found our soulmate. I wasn't hoping, wishing, or praying I had found my soulmate. We both just knew. There are no words I could use to convince others of this, and it wasn't my job to convince them. If I may quote Glennon Doyle one more time, "Every life is an unprecedented experiment. This life is mine alone. So I have stopped asking people for directions to places they've never been. There is no map" (Doyle, 2020).

I knew I was a woman who had done the work (I'm still doing the work). From healing trauma and defining my own spiritual path, to self-reflection through therapy and daily journaling, to reading countless books; I was not the same woman I was a decade earlier. My energy had shifted. Having healed old, self-limiting beliefs, I was physically, mentally, and spiritually ready to enter a healthy, committed relationship.

Just prior to meeting Christian, there was a lovely song I used to listen to by Beautiful Chorus. The song's only chant was, "I see myself in joy and love, I know myself, I am enough."

The first time I listened and sang along to these powerful, succinct lyrics, I cried. Alone in my car, I cried as if those tears were forging a path in my soul to open the way for more joy and love in my life. I cried because I finally knew, "*I am enough.*"

This, dear friends, is why, like the legendary phoenix, I emerged from the ashes of my former life vibrating on a higher frequency. I know the healing path I traveled paved the way for Christian into my life. I deserve to be cherished. I deserve to love and be loved deeply in this life, and once I had found that love, the entire world could whisper in disapproval, and I would not be moved.

Theology

"The important thing is not to stop questioning. Curiosity has its own reason for existing. One cannot help but be in awe when one contemplates the mysteries of eternity .... Never lose a holy curiosity."

— Albert Einstein

My gradual spiritual awakening started in college when I first began to study theology. I grew up in a rigid and demanding Pentecostal church with a strict, literalistic view of God and the Bible that put God in a narrow box. It was not safe to venture outside of that box. The consequence was eternal damnation.

Among the eternally damned were not just "non-believers" and those of other religions, but even Christians who weren't really knocking it out of the park. One had to get it *just right*, which meant the vast majority of the world was on AC/DC's infamous "Highway to Hell."

Let's just say it wasn't the ideal environment to develop my worldview as a child. To be sure, God's grace was definitely brought up in song and sermon, but holding on to that grace was like trying to hold on to a slippery life preserver out at sea in the middle of a hurricane. It never felt all that secure.

In college I started studying the theology and history of the New Testament as well as Eastern religions. That lit a spark of curiosity inside of me, and I went on after college to deepen my learning and understanding even further. What I loved about studying the theology of Christianity is the freedom that came from learning that the narrow viewpoint from which I had been taught the meaning of scripture was not the *only* way to interpret scripture, and that the traditional evangelical version of Christianity is actually quite new and doesn't necessarily align with what early Christians believed. Christianity has changed *a lot* since Jesus lived. This allowed me to begin approaching my beliefs with a healthy level of flexibility and curiosity … *voilà*! God was now safely outside the box.

Over the years I have studied other faith traditions outside Christianity and gotten to know people of other faiths and cultures. If you've ever personally witnessed the authenticity of another person's spiritual experience that is different from your own, then you know that no one has the right to judge another's spiritual path.

My personal view of the sacred can be described with a beautiful analogy about water. Think of God like water deep within the ground, and think of religions like the wells that connect us to water. In the same way wells connect us to water, so do religions and spiritual practices connect us to God—different wells, same water. Like wells reaching down for the water, so do our diverse faiths connect us to that same sacred source.

The late Bishop John Shelby Spong could not have stated it more simply or elegantly when he said, "God is not a Christian, God is not a Jew, or a Muslim, or a Hindu, or a Buddhist. All of those are human systems which human beings have created to try to help us walk into the mystery of God. I honor my tradition. I walk through my tradition, but I don't think my tradition defines God, I think it only points me to God."

I was recently at the hospital for some medical tests and the registration clerk asked if I would like to mark down a religious preference, and for the first time I confidently told her, "No thank you."

This once would have been too dangerous a leap for me to make because, as I mentioned, any coloring outside the lines was met with threat of eternal damnation.

When I say "no" to a specific religion, I'm not saying "no" to God. Remember, my God is the source, as vast as the big, beautiful ocean. Checking a box in my medical chart feels like trying to pour my ocean into a little bucket. My faith is so much more. It can't be confined to or defined by a checkmark on a piece of paper.

I've also increasingly distanced myself from a label because of how politicized the church has become. The crystal-clear water has become muddied with bigotry against homosexuality in the name of God. The church has become too cozy with American patriotism and nationalism. There is nothing wrong with being a patriot, but Jesus was Jewish, not American.

Many of my friends and family are still deeply religious Christians. We both share a love for Jesus. I honor and respect their experience with their beloved faith and its traditions and recognize the positive impact it has in their lives.

My personal relationship with God has outgrown the churches I've attended. That does not mean I think of myself as any better or less than those still sitting in the pews. Each person's spiritual path is theirs to walk, and none of us have the authority to judge another's path as right or wrong.

Whether you are religious, spiritual, atheist, or agnostic, I think there is always some kind of spiritual component to healing. As the priest and French philosopher Pierre Teilhard de Chardin remarked, "You are not a human being having a spiritual experience. You are a spiritual being having a human experience."

Redefining my spirituality was one of the biggest pieces of my healing journey. As I mentioned earlier, the stringent religious environment I grew up in left me with some pretty dysfunctional subconscious beliefs, and a major part of healing was uncovering these beliefs that had been running undetected under the surface but were still driving my anxiety. Slowly, over a period of years, I had been peeling back layers of beliefs, discovering what lived in the shadowy parts of my consciousness. Things can get a little messy when you start diving into the shadows, but that's the thing about shadows —things remain hidden in the dark until you bring the light to them.

Born Again

"Then he said, 'I tell you the truth. You must change and become like little children. If you don't do this, you will never enter the kingdom of heaven.'"

— Matthew 18:3, ICB

There is a freedom that comes in doing the deep, challenging work of healing from our pasts, even if on the surface there doesn't seem to be anything from our past that could still be hurting us. My childhood wasn't perfect (spoiler alert—no one's is), but I had a good childhood with loving parents. I am one of the fortunate ones, and still I developed self-limiting beliefs and unhealthy patterns.

That's just what life does from the moment of our birth. Society, our culture, family, our schools, our peers, and institutions—they imprint things upon us, and gradually we accept these imprints as truths of our own. It's not that all these core beliefs we develop are somehow bad. It's that this all happened without our choosing, and now you're an adult and you get to choose. How much of this stuff would we have willingly chosen if we had the ability from a young, impressionable age to make such kinds of decisions for ourselves? How much of this "stuff" we're carrying is who we really are?

About three years ago I was on my way to work thinking about the story in the book of Matthew where Jesus says if you want to enter the kingdom of heaven, you must become like a little child. It suddenly hit me that morning that this is our life's work—to uncover all the stuff, the imprints and stories and experiences that have shaped us into something other than our true selves. When we strip it all away, what we are left with is that child we once were, pure and untouched, and the kingdom of heaven opens to us.

Holiness or wholeness, therefore, isn't about being born inherently *bad* and penitently striving to become *good*. It's about recognizing our inherent *goodness*. It's a stripping away of what the world has imposed on us and returning to that part of us that has always been whole. To borrow a term popular with evangelical Christianity, I guess you could even say it is becoming *born again*.

When it comes to our love lives, I share all of this because regardless of what you believe, so many of us keep attracting the wrong kind of partner, and another large group of us do have a good partner, but we haven't healed our emotional history and so we unwittingly keep hurting the ones we love. Some of it is generational trauma and not even our own trauma. Either way it is madness. We must do better. We need to heal so we can stop hurting those we are trying to love. We need to heal so we can open ourselves up to and experience the kind of divine love that is our birthright.

When I discovered my subconscious beliefs about "not being enough," when I got to the root of my perfectionism and people-pleasing, when I healed old wounds and traumas, when I opened myself up to being cherished and declared *I see myself in joy and love, I know myself, I am enough,* I cleared a path to receiving the kind of love I had always wanted.

World-Class Hugs

Within the first seven months of 2020, I had moved twice, had a major surgery, ended a marriage, and found my soulmate. All this, while COVID-19 completely and suddenly changed the way we all lived. I was happy and hopeful, but physically drained.

In the same way my well-behaved four-year-old suddenly has a complete meltdown once he gets home from a long day of preschool, it's as if the moment I got into an emotionally safe space, my body unleashed a major meltdown as well. My nervous system had switched to "fight or flight" mode, and I could hardly eat or sleep. My heart was constantly racing, and anytime I got behind the wheel of my car, I had such a massive panic attack it felt like I was going to lose consciousness.

I had two young boys I was trying to put my best face forward for. They too had been through a considerable change, and although they were handling it amazingly well, I wanted to make their transition into a two-home family as positive as possible, but my anxiety was making it exceedingly difficult to even get through normal daily life. This was the physically sickest I'd ever felt for a prolonged time period. My nervous system had been through enough and it was done sending me subtle hints to get me to slow down.

There's a time to be strong and independent, and there's a time to ask for help. The asking for help part has always been difficult for me. This is where I put Christian's promise to show me who he really is with both words and actions to the test.

I scheduled an appointment with my doctor, because I knew at this point I needed medication. I have lots of beneficial coping skills for stress, but this was beyond that. My body was in a state of crisis, and my gut told me that I needed the help of modern medicine to give my body relief.

The 30-minute drive to the doctor's office might as well have been thirty hours. The last time I'd driven before that

I had to pull over and ask my dad to meet me somewhere because I felt like I was going to pass out. So, I swallowed my pride and called Christian to ask him to drive me to my appointment.

This required him to drop what he was doing that morning, drive thirty minutes to my house, thirty minutes to my doctor's appointment, wait with me for over an hour to be seen, and then wait some more while I was being seen, before driving me back to my house. Without hesitation or complaint, he did that for me. He pulled up in my driveway like a gallant knight riding in on his white stallion—ok, ok, it was a white Kia Forte, but you get the idea.

My mind was enveloped in a thick layer of brain fog as I made each labored step down the dilapidated concrete sidewalk towards the entrance of the doctor's office. When I finally sat down in the exam room, my resting heart rate was racing at 120 beats per minute, my cortisol levels were clinically elevated, and my pupils were dilated, giving me the appearance of a frightened animal. This was me at my worst. Normally we wait a few years to make our romantic partners make good on that "for better or worse" deal, but here I was showing my worst early on, and Christian absolutely stepped up to the challenge.

Thankfully, a short-term beta blocker and an SNRI were just what I needed to calm my nervous system and ease my body's stress response, but you know what else is amazing for stress? Oxytocin. Known as the love hormone, research tells us oxytocin's effects are basically the opposite of those linked to our fight or flight response. This too was exactly what the doctor ordered.

Oxytocin is a neurotransmitter released in the brain during labor, breastfeeding, sexual activity, and positive social interactions. I won't specify which method of delivery I was getting, but I *will* say I was getting it in mega doses. I was getting my daily double, sometimes even triple, dose of it, and I will say no more about that (wink, wink).

In all seriousness though, one of my favorite things about Christian are his world-class hugs. They are as tight as an anaconda squeeze and make you feel safe and grounded all at once. I'm not talking about the kind of polite, one-arm side hug you give to your distant relatives at the end of a yearly family gathering. I'm talking about a full-on blood-pressure-cuff love squeeze that melts any tension away. It's not just the intensity; it's the duration. Not that I've ever timed it, but his hugs aren't in a hurry either, which is nice because according to science a hug that lasts twenty seconds is long enough for our brains to release oxytocin (Grewen et al., 2003), that wonderful love hormone that relaxes our bodies and eases anxiety.

Second Chances

"You can change or stay the same, there are no rules to this thing. We can make the best or the worst of it. I hope you make the best of it. And I hope you see things that startle you. I hope you feel things you never felt before. I hope you meet people with a different point of view. I hope you live a life you're proud of. If you find that you're not, I hope you have the courage to start all over again."

—Often attributed to F. Scott Fitzgerald

There is a certain kind of gratitude that comes with second chances. Like near death experiences that lead to living life more fully, sometimes love is that way. There are those fortunate souls who go on to marry their high school sweetheart and happily live out the remainder of their lives together. They have figured out that ever-elusive concoction to weather the good and bad times together, and ultimately grow up and grow old together. I know a handful of these people, and their love story is so pure and beautiful. I'm thankful love stories like this exist, and then there is the rest of us.

If you've made it this far in the book, you already know I'm not one of those stories. From my earliest dating experiences, I never really understood why I seemed to be so unlucky in love. Even in high school my boyfriend dumped me right before senior prom. Then I went on to date a few non-committal assholes in college. I had a long-distance relationship right out of college that had potential, but literally and figuratively couldn't go the distance. Then I met someone who made me feel loved with whom I shared a great spark, but that spark wasn't enough to make him want to marry me. A year and a half into the relationship, he broke my heart.

It was when I was still mending that broken heart that I met my first husband. It seems surreal to say "my first husband" because I never thought I would be one of those people who has to refer to someone as my first husband, *sigh*, but I guess then again who does?

I'm grateful for all the experiences I've endured in my past because ultimately, they landed me in the exact right time and place to meet Christian. But these failed attempts at love were not just stepping stones to Christian; they were more than that. Having experienced exactly what I don't want love to be, I'm able to appreciate and cherish the love that I have now more deeply.

Because of the failure and pain Christian and I both experienced prior to meeting each other, we will never take each other for granted. There is a deep and unshakable appreciation between the two of us. It's like every day I still have this moment of, *I can't believe this is my real life now*, and yet it is, and I know how truly lucky I am.

My wish for anyone reading this book is, if not now, someday you will also look back at the missed attempts, the hurt, and the failures, and you will be filled with gratitude for how these experiences led you to the exact divine place where you need to be.

When Two Givers Indulge in a Connection

What exactly is this great love I'm speaking about? What makes it so special? I can't speak for anyone else's experience, but I know for me, it's a love that keeps my cup overflowing. There's no special formula that makes a great relationship. It's not the number of times he or she buys you gifts or says "I love you." It's not the number of times you have sex every week or how many cool trips you go on together as a couple. If you're familiar with *The 5 Love Languages* by Gary Chapman, people seem to lean towards expressing and receiving love in different ways (Chapman, 2010):

- Words of affection/affirmation
- Physical touch like hugs, hand holding or sexual intimacy
- Spending quality time together
- The giving and receiving of gifts
- Doing things for the other person, also referred to as "acts of service"

The concept of love languages makes a lot of sense to me, because when you can't or won't "speak" your partner's love language, then the other person often feels unloved and unappreciated. Conversely, learning to speak your partner's preferred love languages is a wonderful way to enrich and improve your relationship. However, *I don't think love languages alone are the complete answer.*

I think the secret might just be lying underneath the surface of all this, and I think it's the emotional well-being of each individual in the relationship. When two emotionally healthy adults enter a relationship, one love language may come more naturally than another, but they are able to speak in all five love languages. *They are multilingual in love.*

Past hurts aren't making it impossible for one partner to be affectionate. Grudges and resentment aren't hampering one's ability or willingness to provide acts of service for their loved one. Unresolved traumas aren't making it difficult for one of the partners to be physically touched.

I have an annoying coffee maker. It was a lovely wedding gift and makes delicious coffee concoctions, but half the time it doesn't work like it's supposed to. I make sure there's water. I put the coffee in, I press the power button, and I wait for the coffee to flow. Half of the time the coffee doesn't flow because there is something wrong with this coffee maker.

My coffee maker is like a lot of people. There is something wrong blocking the flow, not of coffee, but of love. We must address the root cause of the issue, otherwise the love we are all capable of doesn't flow through us to the other person.

When a person is emotionally healthy and has addressed any malfunctioning parts (unlike my coffee maker), the flow is beautiful. What the receiving partner ends up with is a full cup. That is why it is so important that both partners are willing to do the healing work that I speak about throughout this book.

I believe individuals who are fluent in all five love languages are also what we commonly refer to as "givers." Showing love in many ways just comes naturally for givers, and once again, this boils down to emotional well-being. Emotionally toxic relationships rarely consist of two givers. Instead, these relationships consist of a taker and a giver (to their own detriment). I'm reminded of Billy Chapata's beautiful quote I came across on social media that reads, "When two givers indulge in a connection, it's magic. It's alchemy. I water you. You water me. We never drain each other, we just grow."

I think that's the secret for Christian and me. We are both givers. We give fluently in all the love languages. I cook meals for us, he does the dishes (acts of service). We hold hands in the car. He gives world-class hugs, and I scratch his back each night as he falls asleep (physical touch). He regularly reminds me how beautiful I am, and I tell him how much he has changed my life for the better (words of affirmation). When he goes to the store, he remembers to bring home dark chocolate, and when I see peanut butter-flavored anything, I scoop it up because I know how obsessed he is with peanut butter (gifts). We make time for each other whether it's a weekend of glamping and hiking or just a lunch break where we sit and binge watch TikTok videos (quality time).

The love he gives me daily makes me a better wife. I'm a better wife because my cup is full, and I'm able to continuously pour from the overflow. The kids can sense this air of respect and love in the home and will benefit in the long-term from the example of a healthy, committed relationship we are showing them, because the foundation that we lay will be the blueprints in which they make decisions around love in their own future.

I'm not trying to create an unrealistic picture of perfection. Yes, we have disagreements and misunderstandings. Yes, the stressors that go along with having a blended family can get the better of us at moments. We say things, and after we say them, we immediately regret it, but we've never once questioned if the other truly loves or appreciates us. This is because we have made enough deposits into our hypothetical "love account" that an occasional withdrawal does not overdraft our relationship.

I'm reminded of an aspect of John Gottman's research, which focuses on the ratio of positive to negative interactions between couples. The magic ratio for happy couples is five to one. This means for every negative feeling or interaction with your partner, there must be at least five positive feelings or interactions (Benson, 2022). For couples like Christian and I who are multilingual with our love languages, this becomes an effortless ratio to maintain. Our everyday stressors are balanced with plenty of compliments, physical connection, time spent together, small favors done for one another, etc.

No doubt all relationships will be sprinkled with both good times and bad. That's part of the "for better or for worse" agreement; However, "for better or for worse" does not mean we tolerate bad behavior from our partner at any and all costs. There is a major difference between the inevitable heartache life brings through unpredictable loss, grief, illness, and misfortune, and the heartache that comes from a partner who neglects, mistreats, cheats, or belittles you. A "for better or worse" promise does not mean you are obligated to tolerate mistreatment, manipulation, or abuse. Your partner should be your life preserver and your safe place from the storms of life, not the storm itself.

Keeping Score Is for Sports Not Marriages

Christian and I want our relationship to continue to be focused on giving to one another. So, what we've consciously excluded from our relationship is "scorekeeping." Keeping score seems to come so naturally that even children become obsessed with it from an early age. For my two boys, virtually anything can turn into a contest—who can run to the mailbox the fastest, who can finish dinner first, who has more Fruity Pebbles in their bowl, etc., etc. On it goes until my hair eventually turns totally gray.

However normal and natural it may be, I'm convinced scorekeeping is absolutely toxic in a marriage. If we look at scorekeeping from the lens of "givers vs takers," there is actually a third archetype at play, "matchers." On a surface level being a matcher seems to make sense. After all, we are taught an ideal modern marriage should be 50/50, right? But that is nearly impossible to track and enforce. Where does the 50/50 concept apply? Is it applied strictly to the division of household labor? Does it also apply to parenting? What about how much physical intimacy you give your partner? Do you each initiate sex only half of the time? What happens if I'm in the mood, but I initiated last time?

Beyond how absurd it is to try to maintain an actual 50/50 relationship, the scorekeeping quickly becomes toxic because how much effort you put into a relationship is entirely subjective, and if I only want to give as much to the relationship as I see my partner contributing, then I'm always calculating my next move. We become defensive as we each try to get the other to see our contribution to the relationship as "enough," as maybe even "more than our fair share." We may even downplay our partner's contribution so we can win, because where there is scorekeeping, there is bound to be a winner and a loser. Scorekeeping leads to cynicism and resentment— one small cut at a time.

I have been there, and I don't ever want to be inside of that kind of relationship again. Some days we catch ourselves teetering on the edge of a scorekeeping interaction, and one of us will say out loud, "I don't want to keep score." We get it, we stop ourselves.

The antidote to a 50/50 relationship is a 100/100 relationship—not "giver and taker," not "matcher and matcher," but "giver and giver." When both lovers give fully to the relationship without holding back, without calculating scores, the beauty is that there is a certain kind of safety to that. We go to the deep end of the pool, we count to three, and we both jump. We're both all in. We're smiling and laughing at the others at the pool. They are slowly and begrudgingly easing their way into the water, half in, half out, freezing, and miserable. Find you a partner who will hold your hand and dive all the way in.

Take Back Your Power

I can be a lot. I feel all the feelings. I am heatedly passionate about causes that are important to me. I love learning so much that in the year 2019, when I first subscribed to Audible, I sped through forty non-fiction audiobooks during my commute to work. I'm a research nerd. I study psychology, health, neuroscience, theology, permaculture and all things self-improvement. I'm spiritual, but my spiritual beliefs don't fit neatly into any of the prefabricated boxes.

When I first started contemplating the possibility of being single again, I told myself I would be too much for most men. I mean, things like implicit bias, the role of the amygdala in fear, or the diversity of your microbiome don't exactly make for great first date conversation. I mistakenly thought it would be pretty difficult to find a man who could handle me emotionally, intellectually, and spiritually.

As Christian and I were getting to know each other, he was proving to be a good match for me intellectually, and he handled the alleged "too much" parts of me quite well. As a well-known local rapper, I discovered in reality he's a lyricist, a researcher, writer, and poet. His brain works impossibly fast. He can freestyle about anything with absolutely no preparation, and a lot of his work contains really deep stuff—stuff you wouldn't expect to hear about in a hip-hop song.

For example, I was listening to his music and there was a line in one of his songs saying something like, "More controversial than the Gospel of Mary Magdalene." I was secretly geeking out because at the time I was reading *Mary Magdalene Revealed* by Meggan Watterson, a book that deeply explores the feminist gospel and Christianity of Mary. Hearing his song only confirmed, "Yes, maybe this guy *can* handle me!"

A couple of months into our romantic relationship, I decided to test the waters a little bit. We were on a picnic at a local park, and I was sharing with him about a recent experience I had in my women's circle. There was a guided meditation where we envisioned going into a cave, and within the cave was a circle of women who would impart a special piece of wisdom, an important message. (Maybe I've already lost some of you at the mention of metaphorically entering a cave.)

I envisioned all the women who meant something to me, both alive and those who had already passed on from this life. In my vision-like meditation, a friend who had just passed away was there. She stepped forward with a message for me, and she told me to "take back my power."

Later in the ceremony, after the meditation, I pulled an oracle card from the center of our circle. I pulled the card representing protection. I was struck with awe as I read the card. After just having received the message in my meditation about taking back my power, the first line on my card read, "Call back your power, cut the cords, soul retrieval."

The card's message urged me to protect my energy and call back my power by looking at who and what drains my energy.

When we worry more about what others think of us than what we think of ourselves, we hand over our power to something or someone outside ourselves. It is true I had spent too much time giving my power away, draining my energy by worrying about what others think of me, and trying to please others at my own expense.

It was such a special moment and message for me, I wanted to share it with Christian. After relating my experience to him, I tentatively asked if he would let me pull an oracle card for him from my own deck. To my surprise he was open to it.

I led us through some deep breaths and a centering prayer and asked him to pick one of the forty-four cards lying face down in front of him. Without hesitation, he decisively grabbed a card, flipped it up, and to our amazement it was the same exact "protection" card I was just telling him about.

We were momentarily speechless. 1 in 44 odds aren't astronomical by any means, but it was enough to send chills down our spines. Even if it took nearly half of our lives to find each other, we both were on this journey together, and at the same time, we seemed to be each other's destination. We both had been on a path in our lives of letting others drain us of our power and energy, and together we were choosing to take our power back.

Sensitive, caring people (sometimes referred to as empaths or highly sensitive people) tend to naturally give a lot of our power and energy away without realizing it. Because we can literally feel the emotions of those around us as if they were our own, we empaths tend to spend a lot of time "outside" ourselves, giving our energy away to others. This is neither a good nor bad thing without some context.

To be clear, I'm glad I was gifted with strong empathy for others. Growing up one of my favorite scriptures was Romans 12:15-16: "Rejoice with those who rejoice, mourn with those who mourn, live in harmony with one another." This sounds like a recipe for a beautiful, harmonious life.

On the flip side, for most of my life I believed that living in peace and harmony with one another meant agreeing with one another. The people-pleaser in me viewed conflict or confrontation as a thing to be avoided as much as humanly possible, but when we silence or censor ourselves to keep the peace, we start a war within ourselves. I now prefer the late Martin Luther King Jr.'s peace, which he defined as "not merely the absence of tension" but "the presence of justice."

By all means, rejoice and mourn with your neighbor, but don't fall into the people-pleaser's trap.

Where we empaths can also fall into a trap is when we attract the wrong kind of personality into our life, who will sense our propensity to feel and care for others, and knowingly or unknowingly take advantage of it. Empaths are natural healers and givers, and thus we often appeal to those in need of healing or those who will take from us. Uncoincidentally, if you Google what type of people empaths attract, the first search result points to how empaths may attract those with a narcissistic personality type; however, I don't feel empaths are doomed to this fate. As we heal, our energy shifts and we begin making conscious choices for our greater good.

Four Lungs That Breathe as One

So maybe 1 in 44 odds of pulling the same card out of a deck is not enough to win over any skeptics. How about 1 in 2,500 odds? Because this is the estimated prevalence of Americans with Alpha-1 Antitrypsin Deficiency, an inherited condition that causes low levels of a protein in the blood that protects the lungs. Roughly 1 in every 2,500 people are thought to have this condition (The Alpha-1 Foundation, 2022). It turns out Christian and I both have this rare condition.

Several years ago, Christian discovered his Alpha-1 lung condition by accident when he was hospitalized with a suspected blood clot. I had never heard of this condition until he told me about it, but a couple weeks later as I was browsing the results of some genetic testing I had completed the year before, I did a double take when I scrolled past the part of the report indicating I too had inherited the Alpha-1 gene.

Since there are two of us, that means we are 2 in 5000 people who have this gene. Those are some wild odds, and luckily now that I have this awareness, I can take proactive action to protect my lungs.

Remember that line from the James Blunt song, *You're Beautiful,* where he says, "There must be an angel with a smile on her face when she thought up that I should be with you?"

Somewhere out there I picture a scheming little angel perched up on some star. He is smiling with satisfaction at the perfection, down to the very last detail, that is our two souls together and the miracle that we even found our way to each other in a sea of billions of souls.

So matching lung conditions aren't exactly the stuff that Harlequin romance novels are made of, but I want you to really grasp how your soulmate is meant to be all that and a bag of chips, the cake *and* eating it, the cat's meow, the bee's knees … you get the idea. When I say there is a love out there for you that will exceed all of your expectations, I literally mean that.

One of my top love languages is physical touch, and because of that I have always preferred when dining out to sit right next to my significant other. Even if we are the only two people at the booth or table, I want my partner right beside me. It's just a small gesture that fills my cup. My former partner would not sit beside me at a restaurant if it were just the two of us. I guess he found it embarrassing or socially unacceptable.

Nowadays, when I eat out, not only does Christian sit beside me, but he is also left handed and I am right handed, so elbow room is never an issue. We can sit right next to each other, even hold hands while we are eating. That right there is a custom-fit love.

Don't Marry Potential

I fear right about now someone is sounding the alarm, saying I am setting up unrealistic expectations for love. Perhaps they are right. Because of my personal experience, maybe I'm biased, maybe my expectations are now too high, but I would argue my bar only looks so high to those who have set their bar so low, including pop culture at large. When was the last time you heard a sit-com or stand-up comedian say something positive about marriage? Our culture equates marriage with the demise of passion and romance.

"One should always be in love. That's the reason one should never marry," chides Oscar Wilde.

Groucho Marx adds, "Marriage is a wonderful institution, but who wants to live in an institution?"

It seems even history's most beloved president, honest Abraham Lincoln, held a rather bleak view of marriage as well. "Marriage is neither heaven nor hell, it is simply purgatory," he is quoted as saying.

As far as high expectations go, I may be in the minority, but I'm keeping my bar all the way up here. You can decide where you want your bar to be. Just don't dare delude yourself into believing passionate, loving, fulfilling marriages don't exist, because I'm here to prove otherwise.

Decide what your non-negotiables are for what you want love to look like when it shows up for you. Decide what you can live with and what you absolutely cannot live without. A good rule of thumb before entering into a marriage or other committed relationship is to ask yourself, can you be satisfied with this person exactly as they are, or do you need them to change something about themselves?

The best and most succinct nugget of wisdom I have ever encountered on this topic, as it so often does, came from a quote on a social media post that stopped me dead in scrolling. "Whatever you tolerate while dating will multiply times ten in marriage. Marriage doesn't fix dysfunction; it reveals all of it. Don't marry potential, marry reality," warns Darius McClure.

I am going to say it one more time for those seated in the back. *Don't marry potential, marry reality.* You know what—just to make sure it sinks in, let's all say it together. *Don't marry potential, marry reality.* No matter how many times he or she has promised to change or how badly you want them to change, no matter how many other good qualities they may possess, be brutally honest with yourself. Will you be satisfied in a relationship with your partner exactly as they show up today, *or* is your happiness hinging upon some future change they may or may not even be capable of or willing to make?

I wish someone could have warned me in my mid-twenties that after planning for the wedding, the honeymoon, and then the babies, life comes to a distinct standstill. You will then see with 20/20 vision the person you married. When you have fulfilled the "American Dream," what's left is still the same two people from the beginning. To quote the wonderful late Maya Angelou once more, "When someone shows you who they are the first time, believe them."

Sometimes when our love interest isn't measuring up to our standards, instead of being honest with ourselves about this, we move forward secretly hoping that they will change. We marry potential. Like trying to fit into that pair of jeans two sizes too small, don't delude yourself. Yes, people (and jean sizes) can and do change, but going into a marriage with the expectation or hope that they do change is a red flag.

Red flags are the seemingly *little* behaviors, beliefs, or situations in a relationship that will eventually turn into *big* issues. Keep your bar high. Don't settle, and while you're at it, go ahead and get yourself a new pair of jeans that fit just right. You'll be way more comfortable.

Harry and Sally

Who doesn't, somewhere deep down, adore a good, sappy rom-com? Topping almost any list of best-ever rom-coms is *When Harry Met Sally*. This beloved movie, with its iconic diner scene ("I'll have what she's having"), is my kind of love story. Just like Christian's and my story, it's a little bit messy. Harry and Sally don't live happily ever after with the first person they become engaged to or marry. It's a story of second chances.

I've always had a soft spot in my heart for a love story with a comfortingly predictable happy ending, although as I grew older, I found them harder to watch as the reality sunk in that my chances of feeling that way had passed me by. By the time I reached my early thirties I had accepted that my fate as a mother and wife was a reality depleted of feelings of romantic love.

Harry and Sally didn't fall in love the first time they met in college, but when the time was right, twelve years later, Harry crashes the party and declares, "I came here tonight because when you realize you want to spend the rest of your life with somebody, you want the rest of your life to start as soon as possible."

I get it. After being together for only a few short months, and even despite the fact we had both just been through a divorce, Christian and I would lay in bed, tracing the outline of a wedding ring on each other's ring finger, aching to become husband and wife. Many would think of this as foolish. Many would say, "What's the rush?" But after thirty-six years for me and forty-four years for him, when you *finally* meet the one you want to spend the rest of your life with, you truly do want the rest of your life to start as soon as possible.

Little Black Boxes

When I was going through my divorce, I thought for sure if I met someone, we would cohabitate for a long time before considering marriage. Yet one crisp, cool morning in the fall of 2020, after dating for just six months, we found ourselves wandering into the local jewelry store to "just look" and get some ideas.

About thirty minutes later, we walked out with a black box, and I'm not talking about the kind of black box you find on airplanes. I'm talking about the kind of black box that comes with a complimentary gift bag and tissue paper. The kind of tiny black box that hides comfortably in the back pocket of a gentleman's pants. The kind of little black box that countless trembling hands have surprised the love of their life with—*the* box.

We sat down in the car, momentarily speechless, still both a little shaken at the quickness with which we had made such a major purchase. To commemorate the moment, I whipped out my phone and took a quick selfie before we left the parking lot. Our ear-to-ear smiles in that photo are the only confirmation we needed (as if we needed any) to know we had made the right decision.

It would be a few more months before it was my turn to be surprised with that little black box, but we had already made our decision, ring or no ring.

This time was different for me. I didn't want a *wedding*. I wanted a *marriage* to this man. I would venture to say for many young brides, it's mostly the other way around. They're more focused on throwing a wedding than preparing for a marriage. All the attention goes towards the planning and pageantry of throwing a beautiful wedding in which the bride will be the fairytale princess at the center, but very little time is spent planning for what happens after the first dance.

That's not to say one can't have it all. I *love* attending weddings. I love the build-up to when the bride finally walks into the room. I always cry during the exchange of the vows. I live for food, cake, and dancing. Weddings are my jam, and if, at the end of a kick-ass wedding, two people go home to begin successfully building a life together, then move over hokey pokey because *that* is what it is all about!

Christian and I had both already experienced all the tradition of a proper wedding. We were still in the middle of a global pandemic. This time was different. I wanted nothing more than the sun as our witness, a backdrop of mountains as our altar, and the dirt beneath us as our dance floor. We began secretly plotting our elopement. All the years spent without each other had added up, and so we would begin our countdown to the day we would be married: 4/3/21.

The Notebook

"I am no one special, just a common man with common thoughts. I've led a common life. There are no monuments dedicated to me, and my name will soon be forgotten. But in one respect, I've succeeded as gloriously as anyone who ever lived. I've loved another with all my heart and soul, and for me, that has always been enough."

— Noah, *The Notebook*

Ryan Gosling and Rachel McAdams brought the film adaptation of Nicholas Sparks' *The Notebook* to life, and now the actors are both synonymous with Allie and Noah from the novel. The movie and the book were a smash hit. *The Notebook* is apparently Nicholas Sparks' first published novel, which, as a budding writer myself, I absolutely love. Imagine concocting such an iconic love story for your first ever published work. Wow.

In case you're wondering why I'm still talking about

romantic movies, there is a reason. My previous partner always brought up *The Notebook* to remind me it is fiction—to make sure I knew it is basically smut for desperate housewives, and stories like that most definitely aren't real. I never really understood his constant need to criticize such a widely beloved movie, but I think I get it now. Perhaps it felt threatening.

And he is not alone in how he feels about the story. There is a sizeable majority of others who have dismissed *The Notebook* as unrealistic. In fact, if searching for a quote from the movie, the headline of one of the first search results reads, "15 *The Notebook* Quotes That Are Still Giving Us Unrealistic Expectations for Love."

Maybe it's just easier to dismiss the movie as unrealistic than take personal inventory of why the movie brings up feelings of discomfort or inadequacy. I guess it is easier to believe a love like that is non-existent, rather than to believe it *does* exist, but we don't have it. The urge to not only dismiss romance but to look at it with contempt is a defense mechanism, meant to ensure that we keep our expectations low. If we can be convinced a love like that isn't real, then it is a lot easier for us to tolerate behaviors that don't look or feel very loving.

But what is it that the internet and my ex have against lofty expectations? You get to decide what's real and what's possible for your life. Over the years I lowered my standards of what I expected love to look like until I was secretly ashamed of my reality. That's why, that fateful New Year's Day, my spirit decided enough was enough. I would no longer lower my standards for what I expected from a loving, committed relationship.

When Christian and I got together, he started talking about *The Notebook* too. He's more of a sci-fi, action-movie kind of guy, but of all the movies he would think to bring up to me, of course it was *that* movie. What a fun sense of humor life has. Instead of bringing it up to tell me how ridiculous it is, he brought it up to tell me it reminds him of us. He brought it up not to put it down, but to put it on a pedestal, to show what *is* possible for us if we strive to love each other hard and well through the years, right up until death, just like Allie and Noah did.

Lying in bed one lazy Sunday morning, buried in a fluffy heap of blankets, we did eventually watch *The Notebook* together. Towards the end of the movie I cried, and I wasn't crying just because the end of the movie is poetic and insanely sad. I cried at the juxtaposition of my former life versus my current reality. I cried tears of gratitude. The Allies and Noahs of this world do exist, and we're proof of that.

Maybe you don't have someone in your life to prove to you that what was once impossible is now possible, but I want you to believe it for yourself, nonetheless. Remember, you get to decide where you set the bar. Create the beautiful life you dare to imagine for yourself.

Time

"The distinction between the past, present, and future is only a stubbornly persistent illusion."

— Albert Einstein

Have you ever been to a place, seen a person, or had an experience for the first time, yet somehow on some level it didn't feel like the first time? Some people refer to this as a sense of *déjà vu*. *Déjà vu* is defined as a feeling of already having experienced the present situation. Maybe it's not necessarily having experienced the present situation as much as it is feeling automatically connected to a particular person, place, or thing.

In the summer of 2000, researcher L. Leibovici conducted a study on intercessory prayer and its effects on the outcomes of hospitalized patients with bloodstream infections (Leibovici, 2001). They did find that the group who received the prayer had a significantly shorter hospital stay and a shorter duration of fever compared to the group who did not receive prayer.

This is pretty cool by itself, but there is one fascinating twist to his research—the prayer was offered up four to ten years *after* the patients' hospital stays. You read that right—the study suggests the possibility that prayer offered in the future can affect outcomes now. Or, put another way, praying for something now could impact things that happened in the past.

Does this research support the quantum physics notion that time is not just linear? What if the past, present, and future are how our limited minds perceive time, but what if our perception actually isn't the reality at all?

Our experience of time is in chronological order from start to finish, but what if everything just "is" and time is a construct of our mind? Bear with me here ... I like to think of time as a book. Normally we read a book from first page to last page in that precise order, but the book is already all there. The book just "is." We could just as easily open to any page in the book and read it because the book is already written, even though when we read a book, we typically experience it from start to finish (unless you skip ahead because your heart cannot handle the suspense). Perhaps it's the same with how we experience our lives. Everything already is; we are just experiencing it through the lens of start to finish, the lens of time.

Going back to that moment I shared earlier, when I first recalled locking eyes with Christian: That was the moment I saw my future husband for the first time, except at that time he was a complete stranger, and I certainly was not looking for anyone. Yet without knowing any of what I know now, there was something particularly powerful about that moment I couldn't quite put into words.

To be clear, this wasn't a moment of an attractive stranger catching my eye. I mean, yes, of course my husband is attractive, but I know there have been plenty of times I've made passive eye contact with an objectively attractive individual and totally forgotten about it moments later.

This moment was significant not only because I remember it to this day, but because it gives me pause to wonder, *What else was at work that day?* Was there some kind of crack in the system of linear time which allowed some part of my consciousness to recognize this person, who I had not yet encountered, as the one who I would spend countless future moments with? Could that be the spark of recognition I felt without being able to adequately put my experience into words?

Like the great Persian poet and Sufi master Rumi uttered roughly eight hundred years ago, "The minute I heard my first love story, I started looking for you, not knowing how blind that was. Lovers don't finally meet somewhere. They're in each other all along."

Like the pages of a book that had already been written, had we been in each other all along?

Part III: Bloom

The average temperature in Colorado Springs, Colorado, during the month of April is 44 degrees Fahrenheit. Today is just barely April at that, yet somehow the sun is shining, and it is bewilderingly warm at 75 degrees. We just missed a massive snowstorm by about a week. How lucky are we?

We knew it was a gamble picking a date in early April to elope in the mountains, but if one is getting married in the year 2021, how can you not pick the date 4-3-21? It's as if our whole lives we've been counting down to this moment … 4, 3, 2, 1. The only thing left after "1" is "0"—the shape of a circle, the shape of the rings we will exchange later today. This is a countdown to our sacred moment ending with the circle and all that it represents: wholeness, original perfection, eternity, timelessness.

Joining us is our friend, Byron, the one responsible for getting us together to film the *Truth Hurts* video, and our amazing photographers, Meg and Kevin. Bryon surprised us by getting ordained and booking a flight to Colorado about three weeks ago. Meg and Kevin are as much elopement planners as photographers and made it possible for us to have an elopement in a place we have never visited before.

So here we stand in the Garden of the Gods as the sun starts its patient descent towards the snow-capped top of Pikes Peak, surrounded by towering red rock formations forged three-hundred million years ago.

We are standing beneath the Siamese Twins rock formation, which is just far enough away from most of the people that have gathered at the park on such a beautiful day. Byron's voice, the commanding voice of a spoken word poet, reverberates off the surrounding rocks as he commences our ceremony. My left leg trembles under my dress, but I am not nervous. I am focused, intently present.

My eyes dart back and forth between Byron—because I want to soak in everything he is telling us—and Christian, because when I catch his eye there is a smile behind his eyes that says, "This is finally, actually happening."

Now it is time for me to read my vows aloud. Apart from our photographers, standing back at a distance, there is no one else to hear my invocations. There is no one here to try to impress with eloquent words, just my soulmate, and for the years to come, when I recall this moment, all I will see is his face.

I open the notebook I have been clutching, and after starting off with my favorite Rumi quote, I continue, "The first time I saw you, I felt an inexplicable magnetism, almost a sense of familiarity ... there was something drawing me to you ... and that something is the thing that the poets and the saints alike often write about—that which can't be seen but can only be sensed, like the brush of the wind, the heat radiating from the sun, or the invisible force that holds the galaxies in place. It is the sacred.

"There is no doubt in my mind that the Universe did conspire to bring us together. And if I ever question why we couldn't have found each other sooner, there is only one answer ... we were on our way here to 4, 3 ,2, 1.

"Our love is a sacred gift that I will always safeguard, and I can't imagine a more perfect place to make my vows to you than here and now, with the mountains and the sky as our witnesses.

"When I look into your eyes, I will remember the first time they met mine, and I will always choose to see the best in you.

"Your lips will always bring to mind our made-up songs, and I will continue making songs with you for as long as I have air in my lungs.

"Your arms contain an embrace that melts away my biggest concerns on my worst day, and because of that, my arms are where you will land at the end of each day, where my hands will scratch away any tension from the day.

"I can't forget to mention my favorite part of your body: your big ... heart. I'll never understand what I did to deserve a heart as big and beautiful as yours, but I promise to never take it for granted.

"There are many more parts of you I am enamored with, but I will go ahead and skip down to your feet. I love your feet for how they found me and for where they now stand ... on this sacred ground.

"I'll end with a quote from *When Harry Met Sally:*

"'I came here tonight because when you finally meet the

one you want to spend the rest of your life with, you want the rest of your life to start as soon as possible.'

"Christian Philip Hudson, I love you forever. Let's start the rest of our life together!"

I look up at Christian. His eyes are now glistening with tears. I gesture to hand him the handkerchief that I am holding, as if I'm passing him some sort of baton, as if everything leading up to this moment had been an arduous race, and now we can finally see the finish line.

He begins reading his vows. "It took me forty-four years, but I finally found you. As they do in a theatrical introduction to the love interest, your beauty blocked out everything that surrounded you. Silence slowly drowned out all discussions, compositions, and any sporadic sounds taking place. It was you—who I am undisputedly sure to have shared many past lifetimes with—which took me up to that moment I discovered you in this lifetime. Yet, I still couldn't believe the magnificence I saw in front of me.

"From that moment on, until the day your few words in response to me took place, I dreamed of a life that seemed almost real, yet unattainable. Those limited but important lines shared a moment that will always bring that rush of a fast-paced heartbeat and a feeling of, 'This is really happening, she is speaking to me!'

"From that moment, we have quickly built a firm bond that only proves we have been building on it for many lifetimes over, yet our accomplishments still feel so fresh and rewarding. Now our time has come in this lifetime to physically become a nexus to transcribe the rest of our chapters in this book of life together. Because of that, my love, I promise you I will love you fiercely with every portion of sand that falls through the hourglass of life.

"I promise I will protect you, from the simple short defeats of a bad day, to taking on a whole country, if needed, to provide you safety. I promise to stand next to you, only to stand in front as a shield from any harm, and to only stand behind you to catch you and lift you back up during times of struggle—but always side by side with you on this journey.

"I promise to help raise your sons into the kings that they are and watch as they change the world, and together we will show my daughter the queen she is and to only accept the best that the world has to offer.

"I promise to not only listen, but to be patient, understanding, and to remember all things from us both are rooted in the love we both have built. I promise to assist you in succeeding when it comes to your dreams, hobbies, and goals, as well as encourage you to follow them when you need that extra momentum.

"I promise to show this planet we call home, the challenge it faces, as it competes for the title of 'perfect' with the beauty that stands before me. I promise to cherish each joyous moment we create as well as share in the pain and agony we will encounter on the road we now travel together.

"I promise to value every moment and to never take for granted the amazing bond we have. I promise to show you how lucky I am to have the gift of love, beauty, courage, bravery, and caring all standing by me in the form of my wife.

I promise to stand with you in both the riches of life as well as during the poorest times we may face.

"I promise to share in the pain and sickness we will face and provide all the love needed until we are free of it. I promise you all this, in this lifetime and the next.

"There really aren't any words that have been invented or any treasures worthy of the explanation of how much you truly mean to me. There isn't time enough in this life to show you how important you are. However, I will spend every waking moment searching for words worthy enough and treasures rewarding enough to at least stand a chance to even come close.

"'Time to get those steps in?' were the very first words I was brave enough to utter in your direction. Since then, we have come to this very moment where those words still carry so much meaning. From this day on, 'It's time to get those steps in' as we now walk together, until the next life, where we will pick up where we left off in this lifetime."

Now that he is finished, we anxiously look to Bryon to signal the exchange of our rings followed by the seal of a kiss so we may complete our union.

We finish with just enough daylight to spread our soft blanket over the dry, hard earth and share a slice of cake and a glass of champagne at the Mesa Overlook with a bird's eye view of the distant rock formations and snow-capped mountains.

As dusk settles over this blessedly surreal day, we share our first dance as husband and wife in the dim light. We can't stop smiling at each other. The words to the song we have chosen, Tim McMorris' "Overwhelmed," play out faintly in the background ...

"And from the first glance you gave my world, it slowed, you stopped the time, and in that moment, I could see all of the things that we would be. You were the girl I was waiting for that I'd ask to marry me."

Happily Ever After

It's now been nearly 10 years since I first caught his attention on the big screen. Six years since he caught my eye at the Glassworks building, four since our first conversation, and three years since we spoke aloud our vows that warm spring day on Colorado's red clay soil. To follow the script of every fairytale and romance ever written, we now live happily ever after, right?

I can physically feel the eye rolls and discomfort that the phrase "happily ever after" evokes. Allow me to make a distinction—to say they lived *happily* ever after is different from saying they lived *easily* ever after. Our lives are not promised to be easy, but that does not mean we cannot be fulfilled and content.

I know the healing journey I embarked on several years ago paved a path for my soulmate to make his way into my life, but I want to make it clear that being with my soulmate doesn't free me from having to do "the work." "The work" is our life's work if we want to live free, especially if we dare to strive to live happily ever after.

I constantly and consciously own my story. To continue

along this healing path, I have to be a defensive driver in my own life. I have to remain conscious enough to recognize when old patterns and beliefs are at the wheel. I have to slow down enough to recognize when this is happening and consciously choose how I want to respond.

Christian and I recently taught ourselves how to play chess. Recently while we were playing, I felt he was upset by something that I said. It was a silly disagreement over the rules. He thought I became overly defensive. Even though he insisted he was fine, I couldn't shake the feeling I had somehow upset him and ruined the game. When the game was over, I remained at the table because I literally wanted some time to sit with my feelings.

When I first told one of my best friends about my new relationship with Christian just after my divorce, I remember her cautioning me, because I was so fresh out of an old relationship, to be sure I protected *this* from *that*.

This from *that*—isn't that always the case? Whenever we have a strong emotional reaction to something our partner says or does, we are never *just* being triggered by our partner. We are being triggered by our partner and the thousands of stored experiences in our brain and body that form the circuitry for how we think, feel, and respond to the world around us. So, as it turns out, the old break-up cliché, "It isn't you, it's me," isn't just a line your ex fed you to keep from hurting your feelings; it literally was about him. Or, in the words of Don Miguel Ruiz, author of *The Four Agreements*, "Nothing others do is because of you. What others say and do is a projection of their own reality."

Last night I knew the feelings I was experiencing were not about what had just happened during our game of chess, so I sat there to ask myself, "Where is this coming from?"

But I already knew it was coming from a place of assuming over-responsibility for people's emotions. In a nutshell, somewhere along my path as an empathetic soul, I learned to be responsible for making others happy. This belief was reinforced by my past relationship in which for a decade I tried and failed, despite my best efforts, to make my partner happy. Taking over-responsibility for others' emotions sounds something like, "In order for me to be ok, I need you to be ok," but others' "ok-ness" is not something I can control, nor am I responsible for the moods and behaviors of other people.

I strongly *prefer* those I love and care about to be happy, but it's not my responsibility to make them happy. Sometimes, I know this may come as a shock (insert sarcasm): people are unhappy about something that has nothing to do with *me*! (*Gasps.*) People, including my kids, spouse, friends, family, or the person who just flipped me off in traffic, can be in a bad mood *around* me and that doesn't make their mood *about* me. I still have to regularly remind myself of this fact.

Had I not invested so much time in my own healing, I would have no awareness of my self-limiting beliefs like this. When self-limiting beliefs do show up these days, instead of blindly acting on them, I can choose to respond in a healthier way.

The reasons other people trigger us are as varied and unique as each of our individual experiences are. When you are feeling triggered in your relationships, you can pause and get curious. What belief or experience from your past (imprint) is triggering you? While for me it may be the belief that I'm responsible for other's emotions, for you, it could be that you're feeling powerless, unappreciated, judged, or even abandoned by your partner. Pay close attention—there is almost always a pattern in what you find triggering.

Last night Christian noticed I still seemed upset, so I articulated to him what I was feeling and why. We were able to have a conversation in which neither one of us had to put our guards up and defend ourselves. He gave me a hug, and my whole body softened into that hug, feeling the permission to be my wholly imperfect self.

I have worn the armor of defensiveness in my past relationships. I know how heavy that armor feels—to constantly be on guard, trying to prove my worthiness. It's a losing battle and the armor is too heavy; it weighs me down. The lightness of being held in a partnership where I can bring my whole self, imperfections and all, and still be loved and cherished, and where I can provide the same for my partner—*that* is my happily ever after.

The Path to Healing

"If you should meet your true self in this lifetime, I pray you will recognize you and stay with you forever."
— Jaiya John

On your path to healing the destination isn't somewhere *out there*. It is a journey *inward*. It is our life's work, returning home to ourselves. As the saying goes, "Hurt people, hurt people," but I believe healed people, heal people, which is why I chose to share my story with you.

I want you to heal so that you can truly live. I don't mean be alive in the sense that you have a pulse. I want you to *really* be fully alive—to have the full depth of the human experience, which is not possible if you are blindly living from imprints and unconscious, self-limiting beliefs.

If you haven't set foot on your path to healing just yet, you may be wondering where to start. I don't know what the road ahead looks like for you, but I can tell you the destination is back home to your true self. Pick something, anything, that feels like a step towards your blueprint. God, or as I have grown fond of saying, "the flow of goodness," will guide you towards the help you need. I have found that for every step you take, the Universe takes two steps on your behalf.

So schedule that therapy appointment you've been putting off, set aside fifteen minutes a day to write in your journal, get outside and let the earth nourish your spirit, or join a group of supportive people—to name a few options. Maybe just get still and quiet enough every so often so that you can actually hear your own truth buried inside of you. Surrender. The path will unfold before you, one step at a time. *Look for the synchronicities.*

When you walk this path, things will start happening that "they" have told you are impossible- things like, let's say, *discovering your soulmate.* By now I hope you know how wrong "they" are. When they try and tell you what's real or not real, you will smile and laugh because you know this is your life, not theirs, and you get to decide what is possible for you. I am standing on the sidelines in spirit, cheering you on.

Epilogue

"Our capacity to destroy one another is matched by our capacity to heal one another."

— Bessel van der Kolk

In closing this book, I would like to share some powerful words from Sheleana Aiyana of Rising Woman. I found these words deeply inspiring during a critical time in my healing journey, and I think you will too. These words inspired me to keep listening to my intuition and to keep making tough decisions with the hope it would empower others to do the same.

I want to share my story with as many individuals as possible, and in doing so give others the permission to heal, to let go of what the world expects them to be, and to never, ever dare settle. In the following passage feel free to replace "woman" for "man," or "person," or whatever best suits you.

"Every time a woman listens to her intuition and acts accordingly ... she is leading.

Every time a woman makes a choice that serves her highest good ... she is leading.

Every time you do what's best for you, even when it's hard, even when it's painful, even when it means starting all over, you are leading.

Be powerful sister.

Rise to the occasion.

Every time you honor yourself, you are leading the way for all the women in your community. Women who are watching and maybe even waiting ...

For a sign or source of inspiration ... To leave, to start over, to birth a new dream, to break a pattern, to stand up, to say no more, to say I'm worth it."

— Sheleana Aiyana

It is my most sincere prayer for any soul who comes across my love story that you know you are irrevocably worthy of being loved and cherished. It is also my hope, now that you know what kind of love is possible, you cannot go back to believing that it is not possible.

If you are still searching for the one, I plead with you to not settle for anything less than the kind of love your heart truly desires. Stop searching for the one. Start healing and living your beautiful, blessed life, and let your life lead you to the one. What's for you will not miss you.

I cannot and would not make the decision for another person whether they should stay or leave the relationship they are in. That is not a decision that can or should be made lightly. Every relationship is made up of two imperfect people. Ideally, both of you will commit to owning your stuff, to doing the work, and to healing.

If you're in an unhealthy relationship, I pray it can be restored to health, but if it cannot, you have not failed. You are a human doing the best you can with what you have. Focus on your healing and watch the trajectory of your life change.

If your partner is not willing to come alongside you and put as much love and effort into the relationship as you are, or even worse, if you are being torn down by continuous criticism, don't write it off. Question what place that partnership has in your life—your singular, precious life. Because there are no dress rehearsals, and we don't get a second chance at it. We only get so many years to revolve around the sun on this beautiful planet, and how we spend it matters. How we spend it leaves ripples that will stretch into future generations.

Throughout this book, seeds have been planted in your mind and heart. Now it is up to you to see to it that they grow. A seed must grow through darkness and rain while it awaits the sun. There eventually will be flowers. *You will bloom.*

I recently went back and watched the series finale of *The Office,* and there was this moment where it felt as though Pam Halpert, in her own subtle way, summarized why I wrote this whole book:

> It's just hard to accept that I spent so many years being less happy than I could have been. Jim was 5 feet from my desk, and it took me four years to get to him. It'd be great if people saw this documentary and learned from my mistakes. Not that I'm a tragic person. I'm really happy now. But ... it would just ... just make my heart soar if someone out there saw this and she said to herself, "be strong, trust yourself, love yourself. Conquer your fears. Just go after what you want and act fast because life just isn't that long."

Finally, please see the "Helpful Resources" section at the end of this book for suggested resources to get you started (or to keep you going) on your healing journey. I'm so grateful you picked up this book, and I was able to share my story with you. May it inspire healing and happiness on your path.

XO,

Devon

References

The Alpha-1 Foundation, 2022. https://www.alpha1.org

Benson, Kyle. "The Magic Relationship Ratio, According to Science." The Gottman Institute, 2022. https://www.gottman.com/blog/the-magic-relationship-ratio-according-science/

Brittle, Zach. "R is for Repair." The Gottman Institute, 2022. https://www.gottman.com/blog/r-is-for-repair/#:~:text=Remember%20that%20a%20repair%20attempt,what%20will%20work%20for%20you.

Chapman, Gary D. *The 5 Love Languages*. Walker Large Print, 2010.

Cherwa, John. *Kentucky Derby 20ard19 winner:* "Country House wins after Maximum Security is disqualified." *Los Angeles Times*, 2019. https://www.latimes.com/sports/more/la-sp-kentucky-derby-live-updates-odds-results-start-time-20190504-story.html,

Woodward Thomas, Katherine. *Conscious Uncou-*

pling: 5 Steps to Living Happily Even After. Harmony Books, 2015.

Doyle, Glennon. *Untamed.* The Dial Press, 2020.

Grewen KM, Anderson BJ, Girdler SS, Light KC. "Warm partner contact is related to lower cardiovascular reactivity." *Behav Med.* 2003 Fall;29(3):

Johnson, Kimberly Ann. *The Call of the Wild.* HarperCollins Publishers, 2021.

Kolber, Aundi. *Try Softer: A Fresh Approach to Move Us out of Anxiety, Stress, and Survival Mode-- and into a Life of Connection and Joy.* Tyndale House Publishers, 2020.

Leibovici L. "Effects of remote, retroactive intercessory prayer on outcomes in patients with bloodstream infection: randomised controlled trial." BMJ, 2001.

Nagoski, Emily & Amelia. *Burnout: The Secret to Unlocking the Stress Cycle.* Ballantine Books, 2020.

Perel, Esther. *Mating in Captivity: Unlocking Erotic Intelligence.* HarperCollins Publishers, 2007.

Scher, Amy B. Rewiring Your Mind: How to Erase Your Biggest Limiting Beliefs in Minutes. *Conscious Lifestyle Magazine.* 2019. https://www.consciouslifestylemag.com/limiting-beliefs-overcoming/?_sm_au_=iVVZDMTJtvfPJ45QWTW4vK0p3MfC0

Helpful Healing Resources

In addition to the books I have already mentioned and listed in my references, here are some other helpful resources. This is obviously not an all-inclusive list, but rather a curated list of resources I believe could be of benefit on your healing journey, and/or were helpful to me personally. This is only the tip of the iceberg and a jumping off point—there are so many wonderful healing modalities and resources out there. It's all about finding what works for you!

- Find a Somatic Experiencing practitioner: Somatic Experiencing (SE™) is a potent method for resolving trauma symptoms and relieving chronic stress. https://directory.traumahealing.org
- Find an EMDR therapist: EMDR (Eye Movement Desensitization and Reprocessing) is a psychotherapy that enables people to heal from the symptoms and emotional distress that are the result of disturbing life experiences. https://www.emdr.com/SEARCH/index.php
- Journal Speak, Journaling Prompts: https://www.thecureforchronicpain.com/journalspeak
- National Domestic Violence Hotline: https://www.thehotline.org/, 1-800-799-7233
- National Suicide Prevention Lifeline: https://suicidepreventionlifeline.org/, 1-800-273-8255

- *Rewire Your Anxious Brain: How to Use the Neuroscience of Fear to End Anxiety, Panic, and Worry* by Catherine M. Pittman PhD and Elizabeth M. Karle
- *The Anatomy of Anxiety: Understanding and Overcoming the Body's Fear Response* by Ellen Vora
- *The Myth of Normal: Trauma, Illness, and Healing in a Toxic Culture* by Gabor Mate and Daniel Mate
- The Reclamation Collective: Reclamation Collective is committed to holding space for folks navigating Religious Trauma and Adverse Religious Experiences. We hope to support you as you reclaim, or claim for the very first time, your identity, pleasure, and autonomy. https://www.reclamationcollective.com/
- The Wild Woman Project: The Wild Woman Project is at once a philosophy (an invigorating approach to life as a wondrous, often messy, creative project) and a growing movement of courageous, creative, heart-centered (often weird and wonderful) women on a mission to remember, to reimagine what it means to be a woman —untamed. https://thewildwomanproject.com
- *Waking the Tiger: Healing Trauma* by Peter A. Levine
- *The Body Keeps the Score: Brain, Mind, and Body in the Healing of Trauma* by Bessel Van Der Kolk, M.D.
- *The Inner Child Workbook: An 8-week Guided Adventure to Heal Trauma and Create Inner Safety* by Evelyn Hale, MPA: Reclaim the freedom that was taken from you through complex trauma and adverse childhood experiences. Whether you had Big T or little t trauma, this inner child workbook will guide you to connect

to your inner child and heal through creative activities, journaling prompts, meditations, and rituals.